SHORT CUTS

INTRODUCTIONS TO FILM STUDIES

T0311473

THE VAMPIRE FILM

UNDEAD CINEMA

JEFFREY WEINSTOCK

WALLFLOWER

LONDON and NEW YORK

A Wallflower Press Book
Published by
Columbia University Press
Publishers Since 1893
New York • Chichester, West Sussex
cup.columbia.edu

Wallflower Press® is a registered trademark of Columbia University Press

Cataloging-in-Publication Data is available from the Library of Congress

ISBN 978-0-231-162012 (pbk.)
ISBN 978-0-231-85003-2 (e-book)

Book and cover design: Rob Bowden Design
Cover image: *Nosferatu* (1922). Prana Film.

CONTENTS

INTRODUCTION: VAMPIRE CINEMA

This is a book about vampire movies, but it is a book that I am tempted to say almost does not need to be written. This is not because there is not a lot to say about vampire movies, but because a characteristic feature of vampire movies is that they do the saying themselves. Vampire movies, as we shall see, endlessly and in so many ways talk about vampires and vampire movies. Consider this description of the vampire from 'forensic psychiatrist and biochemist' Dr Edgar Vance (John Michael Higgins) in the third offering from the Wesley Snipes' *Blade* franchise, *Blade: Trinity* (2004): vampires are 'creatures that are the repositories of some of our most taboo thoughts – predatory rage, sexual sadism. These are very scary subjects for people to own up to and they're right inside.' Dr Vance goes on to add that, 'This business of vampirism has a very strong element of sexual confusion. Nuzzling into someone's neck, a nocturnal visit that promises a delicious sexual intimacy.' Even though the movie winks at the audience during this dissertation on vampires, depending upon the spectator's awareness that vampires within the world of the film are real and not simply fantastical projections of repressed sexual desire, the film itself has attempted to theorise on a metatextual level the allure of the vampire.

But there is more. *Blade: Trinity* not only theorises the psychoanalytic etiology of vampires but, in keeping with vampire cinema tradition in general, is also hyper-aware of itself as a vampire film that both conforms to and departs from the sedimented conventions of that tradition – a lineage that can be traced back along a path that runs through the UK's Hammer Studios productions with Christopher Lee, Peter Cushing and Ingrid Pitt to

Universal Studios' classic vampire releases with Bela Lugosi, Gloria Holden and Lon Cheney Jr, and ultimately back to the vampire cinema Ur-text, Bram Stoker's novel *Dracula* from 1897 which, despite not being the first literary vampire story, nonetheless forms the basis for the Platonic vampire ideal, the original from which everything else is copied. Indeed, *Blade: Trinity* actually loops back around to Stoker's text by featuring Dracula (Dominic Purcell) himself – albeit, a revised Dracula: a Dracula, called Drake for short, for the 1990s who prefers a rippling muscled physique (he can assume whatever form he likes) and who can be traced back over six thousand years to ancient Sumeria. 'Dagon to the Babylonians', this Dracula, as the film explains, is revealed to be the first of his kind, 'hominus nocturna', the vampire patriarch. Stoker, *Blade: Trinity* asserts, did not get things quite right. The vampires in the movie need Dracula because, in contrast to their enervated blood, his is 'pure', unadulterated and virile. He can do what they can't – withstand daylight and transform himself – and their 'vampire final solution', with all its fascist, Third Reich overtones, is to reinvigorate – purify – their blood with his.

Thus, not only does *Blade: Trinity* theorise the vampire for us, but it also intertextually situates itself in relation to other vampire texts. In keeping with much contemporary vampire cinema, the film elucidates clearly how its vampires compare with the popular conception and how they differ. This is a vampire film that has a lot to say about vampires and vampire cinema, which we will see is not at all unusual. And yet for all its metatextual consciousness, the film does not exhaust its own interpretive possibilities (no text ever does); nor is it wholly self-aware and fully cognisant of its own origins. What the forensic psychiatrists and biochemists and various authorities on vampirism in *Blade: Trinity* do not discuss – indeed, what is introduced so carelessly that it can easily slip right under the spectator's radar – is the juicy little tidbit that Dracula in this American film from 2004 is dredged up from his crypt in *Iraq*. This tiny detail, mentioned in passing, punctures the hermetic fantasy seal around the film, allowing history to flood back in. The unstated problematic structuring the possibility of *Blade: Trinity* is thus arguably the American occupation of Iraq, which began in 2003. The film demands that we think of Dracula now not just as a creature of myth and legend, but as a terrorist, a monster imported by a domestic fifth column from the Middle East – from Iraq no less – who can assume any form he likes and is out to destroy the Western way of life. Dracula is a vampire dictator whose master plan is to enslave all mankind. His vampire supporters (who we learn in the first *Blade* movie (1998) worship different gods in ancient settings) walk among us, 'passing' like Drake for human while draining our blood and resources. And, as if this weren't enough, *Blade: Trinity* turns out to be a film about weapons of mass destruction – to counter the vampires' quest for world domination, *Blade: Trinity*'s equivalent of Bram Stoker's Crew of Light, the self-appointed 'Nightstalkers', have developed their own 'vampire final solution', an engineered virus that will wipe out the vampire population entirely. Vampires, it turns out, are monsters deserving neither of sympathy nor charity. It is kill or be killed – a war on terror. Vampires are part of George Bush Jr's axis of evil. We must get them before they get us and in this arms race, all options, including biological and chemical weapons, are on the table.

Blade: Trinity thus exemplifies one of the premises of this study: speculative media – horror, fantasy and science fiction – no matter how seemingly distant from the 'real world' they may appear, are inevitably anchored by history and are the products of converging lines of cultural forces. Even as the theorist within the film, in keeping with the psychoanalytic analysis of Freud disciple Ernest Jones in his *On the Nightmare* (1931) (one echoed by folklorist Norine Dresser in *American Vampires* (1989)), offers an ahistorical interpretation of vampires as disavowed projections of fundamental aggressivity and tabooed sexual desire, the film shows the ways in which desire itself is always inflected and given shape by social circumstances. Although vampires in movies are depicted as quasi-immortal creatures, the vampire cinema shows us that cinematic vampires are inevitably products of their historical moment, and although vampires in films like *Blade: Trinity* may have gone global, the expression of underlying fears and desires concerning sex and race and the human relationship with technology is always local – culturally specific and time-bound.

Be Like Me For a While

But let us switch gears for a moment and consider a less bombastic film. In contrast to the bravado and stylised violence of action vampire films like the *Blade* and *Underworld* series, the 2008 Swedish vampire film and critics' darling *Låt den rätte komma in*, translated into English as *Let the Right One In*, feels small and quiet – and decidedly more local. There are no sword fights, engineered viruses, mythological gods or impossibly sculpted physiques in this movie. Instead, there is Oskar (Kåre Hedebrant), a lonely, scrawny twelve-year-old boy bullied by his classmates and living with his mother in a town near Stockholm. When Eli (Lina Leandersson), a dark-haired, olive-complected vampire with the body of a young girl forever on the cusp of puberty, moves in next door, a strange and unsettling friendship develops as each one learns to protect and care for the other.

Although a very different film than *Blade: Trinity*, *Let the Right One In* nonetheless also theorises for us where vampires come from – and the answer interestingly is very much in keeping with the proposition of *Blade: Trinity*'s Dr Vance that vampires are the product of aggression and sexual confusion. The film begins with Oskar, shirtless, smooth-skinned, pale and androgynous, staring at his reflection in the window, holding a knife and commanding, 'Squeal like a pig, squeal!' A context is soon given for this puzzling order as Oskar is intimidated at school by the local bully who pushes Oskar's nose up, telling him, 'What a good piggy you are'. When Oskar that evening reenacts the confrontation, stabbing a tree with his knife while repeating 'what a good piggy you are', the spectator understands that this is a complex form of role playing in which Oskar, full of both rage at the bully and self-loathing, is killing his tormentor and himself – it is a murder/suicide and it summons the vampire as Eli appears, coatless in the snow, asking Oskar what he is doing. The question seems more for Oskar to consider than for Eli because it appears Eli already knows the answer. Oskar, who keeps a scrapbook of newspaper clippings detailing grisly murders and who demonstrates himself to be an amateur forensics scientist in class when he correctly answers a question about how to determine whether someone died before or during a fire, here in essence has conjured up the vampire with his murderous desire. Later, as Eli counsels Oskar to fight back against those who abuse him, she tells him that the first words she heard from him were 'squeal like a pig'.

Eli is effectively Oskar's empowered alter-ego, the manifestation of his rage and pain and thirst for revenge and affirmation. That we should think of Oskar and Eli as being two halves of a larger whole – as doppelgängers of a sort – is suggested both by their similarities and the ways in which they are complementary. They are similar in being twelve (although Eli explains to Oskar that she has been 'twelve for a long time') and essentially sexless (a quick glimpse by Oskar of Eli while changing suggests that Eli has no

Let the Right One In: Eli, an unusual vampire

sex organs at all – in the book upon which the film is based it is revealed that Eli was in fact a boy, castrated centuries before). And significantly they are both alienated from the rest of society – Eli because of her monstrosity and Oskar due to the benign neglect of parents and authority figures preoccupied with their own concerns and unable to see the violence right before their eyes. In other respects they are complementary: Oskar is literally and figuratively day to Eli's night, fair to Eli's darkness, and Oskar is prey while Eli is a predator.

The thrust of the film thus is toward integration of these two halves or alter-egos. This is made clear when Eli explains that she and Oskar are alike. When Oskar protests that he doesn't kill people, she responds 'you would murder if could, to get revenge'. When Oskar affirms that this is true, she tells him to 'be me for a while' and the pact is sealed with a kiss – a turn of events that seems to propel Oskar into adulthood as he subsequently considers his toys with a degree of distance. He has outgrown them. In the end, Eli comes to Oskar's rescue, destroying the bullies who are tormenting him, and Oskar, who has previously come to Eli's rescue by confronting a daytime intruder in her apartment, in turn becomes her caretaker, filling in for her previous familiar whose tragic end has left her unguarded during the day. The final shot shows them traveling together on a train – Oskar tapping out messages of affection in Morse code to Eli who is confined in a crate by his side.

The spectator's celebration of Oskar's rescue, the destruction of his opponents, and the seemingly happy conclusion must be tempered, however, by the realisation of the implications of the decision Oskar has made. Eli's previous caretaker was a serial killer who murdered children and teenagers and drained them of blood to satisfy Eli's needs. In abandoning the life he has known and choosing to be with Eli, Oskar in essence has made the decision to become a killer. He will literally be like Eli, a vampire who kills and drains people of their blood. In contrast to the typical vampire movie, however, it is not Eli who transforms Oskar into a monster; rather, what the movie shows us is that Oskar was well along the path to becoming a vampire from the very start. What *Let the Right One In* demonstrates, in short, is that it takes a village to make a monster. Oskar is failed by his parents who love him but just as easily forget him and don't really listen to him, his teachers who laugh at his interest in crime narratives and embarrass him in front of his peers, all the other authority figures who fail to intervene and prevent him from being bullied and harassed, and his peers who hurt and humiliate him repeatedly. Whether he will command his victims to 'squeal like a pig' as he sticks them is unknown, but what seems clear is the little boy brandishing the knife at his reflection at the start will turn into a man who uses that knife to take the life of other little boys.

How to Make a Monster

What *Blade: Trinity* and *Let the Right One In*, two very different vampire films, begin to point us toward are the underlying concerns and recurring themes of the vampire cinema which, despite its astounding number of entries (Ken Gelder asserts over three thousand films in his 1996 study) and their impressive variation, arguably is structured by a handful of governing principles that offer some coherence to the category and go a long way toward making sense of this movie monster's remarkable fecundity. The extent to which each individual vampire film embodies and manifests these principles will of course differ, but my argument is that these generalities hold true for the vast majority of films and underlie the hypnotic hold the cinematic vampire has exerted over the Western imagination for over a century.

– Principle 1: The cinematic vampire is always about sex

>> Corollary 1.1: Cinematic vampires are marked by performances of hyperbolic gender
>> Corollary 1.2: Cinematic vampires are inevitably queer

Vampire movies are always, inevitably, about sex on some level – although what each vampire film has to say about sex obviously will vary depending upon time and place. This assertion is the organising premise of this book's first chapter. From the 'vamps' of the Theda Bara school that populated the silent screen to Hammer Studios' lesbian vampires of the 1970s to the leather-clad sexiness of vampire Kate Beckinsale in the *Underworld* films (2003, 2006, 2009), and from the suave sophistication of Bela Lugosi's Dracula to Christopher Lee's animal magnetism to the softer model of contemporary masculine perfection offered by Robert Pattinson in *Twilight* (2008), the power and danger of sex has undergirded and energised the vampire cinema from its origins to the present, and that erotic charge, at least in critic David Pirie's estimation in his book *The Vampire Cinema*, constitutes the films' primary appeal (1977: 6) – and Pirie's assertion is backed up by Dresser's sociological study of vampire literature and movie fans that notes that the 'erotic aspects of the vampire were the most frequently mentioned reasons for this creature's appeal' (1977: 148). Vampires, in short, are undeniably the sexiest of monsters.

The erotic *frisson* of vampire films also clearly illustrates Jeffrey Jerome Cohen's linked assertions in the introduction to his collection of essays, *Monster Theory: Reading Culture* (1996) that monsters are always culturally specific creations that police cultural borders even as they reveal tabooed or repressed desires. Monsters, according to Cohen, are linked to 'forbidden practices, in order to normalize and enforce' (1996: 16) and what cinematic vampires have arguably done for much of their existence is to provide representations of tabooed sexuality in order to establish and reinforce proper sexual roles. Vampires, I think it is fair to say, are quite simply very, very naughty. They are seldom decorously heterosexual, monogamous and respectful partners. Rather, they are polymorphously perverse seducers that, in Richard Dyer's estimation, evoke the thrill of 'forbidden sexuality' (1988: 64). The vampire's 'kiss' on the neck in the dark in the bedroom, generally part seduction and part rape, involves the sexualised exchange of bodily fluids and it is no coincidence that, as Andrea Weiss observes, outside of male pornography, 'the lesbian vampire is the most persistent lesbian image in the history of the cinema' (1993: 84). Vampires are undisciplined forces of desire that exist outside of cultural networks of socialisation. Theirs are bodies that spread out, transform and envelop. Driven by their sexualised thirst, they absorb and devour the life-force of their partners. Vampires are pure Id, libidinal energy incarnate. In Pirie's estimation, vampires care for nothing other than the 'gratification of the senses by physical means' (1977: 6); and this makes them both dangerous and dangerously attractive.

Vampires also lend themselves to the cinema because they are the most *theatrical* of monsters. They are always performing – they must 'pass' for human, disguise their true natures and hide their desires. What the vampire performs furthermore – often to the point of parody – are gender stereotypes. Male vampires, whether the Draculas played by Lugosi, Christopher Lee, Frank Langella or Gary Oldman; or David in *The Lost Boys* (1987), or Wesley Snipes' Blade, or those played by Tom Cruise, Brad Pitt and Antonio Banderas in *Interview With the Vampire* (1994); and on and on culminating in Pattinson's *übermensch* Edward Cullen in *Twilight* are impossibly manly – more manly than any human male. And female vampires from Theda Bara to Barbara Steele to Ingrid Pitt to the porn starlets of Jean Rollin and Jésus Franco to Kate Beckinsale similarly are defined by their hyperbolic materialisation of cultural standards of feminine beauty. They are more womanly – more attractive, more seductive, strangely more *alive* – than any real, living human female.

The result is that cinematic vampires are inevitably queer – that is, they reveal in dangerous and exciting ways the extent to which both manliness and womanliness are always masquerades, inevitably flawed performances of cultural expectations. What the cinematic vampire ironically demonstrates is that the only 'true' man or woman is in fact a monster and the vampire's sexual 'deviance' makes abundantly clear that the categories of 'normal' and 'deviant' are not in any way natural and transhistorical but local, constructed and shifting.

– *Principle 2: The vampire is always more interesting than those who pursue it*

Ellis Hanson notes in his essay on lesbian vampires that the vampire 'is always more appealing and exciting than the men and women who hunt it' (1999: 191). This is because, as Nina Auerbach notes, the vampire, the libidinal monster, is ironically more alive than they – and we – are (1995: 6). This is Slavoj Žižek's Lacanian conclusion as well in *For They Know Not What They Do* when he writes that 'The paradox of the vampires is that, precisely as "living dead", they are *far more alive* than us, mortified by the symbolic network [...] the real "living dead" are we, common mortals, condemned to vegetate in the Symbolic' (2002: 221; emphasis in original). In contrast to 'you or I' – the 'we' who 'vegetate in the Symbolic', positioned by language and culture, forced in so many ways to conform and play our dutiful roles as family members and citizens – the vampire lives for pleasure alone. He or she is a figure of excessive – and thus threatening – enjoyment, an uncanny surplus that transgresses social expectations and highlights the precariousness of gender codes.

That 'vampires never explain' (Hanson 1999: 208) or, I might add, apologise, is wholly in keeping with their status as manifestations of the Id governed only by the pleasure principle. Vampires are imperial, selfish, domineering and intensely physical. Lurking beneath the human façade is pure animalistic energy. The vampire's power and potency (the vampire is driven not just to feed but to reproduce) is both frightening and alluring. In comparison, those who seek to destroy the vampire, the agents of cultural repression, cannot help but seem priggish and impotent (while the vampire is promiscuous, one or two good stakings and the heroes are done). Dreaded and desired in equal measure, the vampire is always sexier, always more interesting, and always more commanding than the forces of cultural stability that seek to expel it, which in part is why we won't let it die.

– *Principle 3: The vampire always returns*

>> Corollary 3.1: Vampirism begins at home
>> Corollary 3.2: The vampire always appears to come from someplace else
>> Corollary 3.3: The vampire is always in motion

Cohen notes that 'No monster tastes of death but once', and adds that, 'The anxiety that condenses like green vapor into the form of the vampire can be dispersed temporarily, but the revenant by definition returns' (1996: 5). But any fan of vampire movies already knows this. The vampire may be staked and/or reduced to ashes by the sun at the end of *El Vampiro* (1957) or *The Horror of Dracula* (1958) or *Count Yorga* (1970) or *Blacula* (1972) or *Fright Night* (1985) or *Dracula 2000* (2000), but all that's needed to bring him back is a little blood, or a voodoo ritual, or perhaps simply the removal of a cross from the cold, non-breathing corpse. And even if the vampire itself is actually destroyed, something of him or her, some trace or essence, invariably survives. The Countess Bathory (Delphine Seyrig) is impaled at the end of the delightful *Daughters of Darkness* (1971), but in the final scene Valerie (Danielle Ouimet) speaks with her voice. In the equally excellent American remake, *The Hunger* (1983), Miriam Bleylock (Catherine Deneuve) may be gone, but Sarah Roberts (Susan Sarandon) seems to have taken her place. Referring to the *Alien* movies, Cohen writes that, 'Regardless of how many times Sigourney Weaver's beleaguered Ripley utterly destroys the ambiguous Alien that stalks her, its monstrous progeny return, ready to stalk again in another bigger-than-ever sequel' (1996: 4–5). Similarly, Dracula may be gone for the moment, but his daughter and son will inevitably emerge to carry on the family business.

The vampire always returns because it is ours, our creation, and we won't let it rest. It is our prodigal son, returning home, bearing with it and giving shape to deep-seated anxieties and tabooed desires that, as Mary Pharr observes, may vary with the times but never simply vanish (1999: 93). To taste the blood of Dracula is thus in a sense redundant because Dracula's blood is always already coursing through our veins. It is also the case, however, that, as Cohen observes, each time the monster returns, it looks somewhat different; each time Dracula is unleashed upon the world, he embodies a new structure of feeling, a different awareness of the world, an altered set of fears and desires. Dracula (Bela Lugosi) in Tod Browning's 1931 version is a suave Old World aristocrat; in *The Satanic Rites of Dracula* (1974), he (played by Christopher Lee) is a corporate C.E.O. concocting a virulent strain of Bubonic Plague. In *Nosferatu* (1922), the monstrous vampire Count Orlok (Max Schreck) is conquered by a woman (Ellen, played by Greta Schröder) who passively surrenders her body to the vampire and martyrs herself in the process; in *Buffy the Vampire Slayer* (1992), the vampire is also vanquished by a woman (Kristy Swanson as Buffy), but a stake-wielding one who is far from passive. America always gets the vampire it deserves opines Pirie (1977: 136). More to the point though, each generation of filmmakers, in America and elsewhere, creates the vampires it desires.

The irony of the vampire cinema, however, is that just as soon as the vampires are created, they are disowned. The slight-of-hand trick played by the vampire cinema – the psychic defense mechanism that allows us to disavow the vampire as our own – is that, despite the fact that the vampire always begins at home, it always appears to be coming from someplace else: from Transylvania, from Iraq, from Africa, from deep space, simply from an ambiguous, unspecified elsewhere. In Stephen Arata's (1977) persuasive article on Bram Stoker's *Dracula*, he argues that the novel embodies Victorian xenophobia and the fear of 'reverse colonization' as England is invaded by the potent, debased other from the East. The fear is Victorian England's, but the vampire is represented as arriving from elsewhere and it is this disavowal of relation and staging of difference that recurs in every adaptation of *Dracula* that has the eponymous Count traveling elsewhere from his castle in Transylvania – to Bremen in *Nosferatu*, to England in most adaptations of *Dracula*, to America as Count Alucard (Dracula oh-so-cleverly spelled backwards, played by Lon Cheney Jr) in *Son of Dracula* (1943). And beyond variations on Bram Stoker, this trajectory holds true for the vampire cinema in general. As Ann Davies observes in her analysis of Guillermo del Toro's *Cronos* (1993), 'most if not all vampire texts dissolve and cross boundaries and borders' (2008: 396), which leads her to conclude that border crossing is a basic convention of vampire narratives. Thus, Dracula brings his curse to China in *The Legend of the 7 Golden Vampires* (1974), while the vampire is imported into Japan in *Lake of Dracula* (1971) in a crate – which is how Blacula arrives in Los Angeles in *Blacula* and how Eli leaves the Stockholm suburbs in *Let the Right One In*. New York City is attacked by immigrant vampires in *Nadja* (1994), *Habit* (1997) and even the comedy *Love at First Bite* (1979), while Barrow, Alaska is invaded by voracious vampires with their own language in *30 Days of Night* (2007). Earth itself is the target of extraterrestrial vampires in *Vampirella* (1996) and any reasonably faithful adaptation of Sheridan LeFanu's 'Carmilla', such as *Crypt of the Vampire* (1964) or *The Vampire Lovers* (1970), has Carmilla mysteriously arriving from someplace else.

On occasion, the trajectory is reversed and rather than the vampire being invited in, the protagonist goes out to meet it. These are tales of unwary or unlucky travelers who find themselves in eerie forests, spooky castles and terrorised villages – or in Mexican bars or on exotic beaches or in space. Dr Andre Gorobec (John Richardson) in Mario Bava's *Black Sunday*

(1960) happens across the tomb of the witch Katia Vajda (Barbara Steele) and reanimates her with a drop of blood from a cut on the hand of his companion, Dr Thomas Kruvajan (Andrea Checchi), while Alan Foster (Georges Rivière) in *Castle of Blood* (1964) accepts a bet that he can't survive one night in a spooky mansion and is taken there by none other than Edgar Allan Poe (Silvano Tranquilli) himself! Michael and Sam Emerson (Jason Patrick and Corey Haim) relocate to vampire-infested Santa Carla in *The Lost Boys* while an escape to Mexico with stolen cash in *From Dusk Till Dawn* (1996) takes a wrong turn at a vampire bar. Gerald and Marianne Harcourt (Edward de Souza and Jennifer Daniel) make an ill-advised trip to the castle of Dr Ravna (Noel Willman) in *The Kiss of the Vampire* (1963), while Linda Westinghouse (Ewa Strömberg) in *Vampyros Lesbos* (1971) is sent by her firm from Budapest to an exotic Anatolian island and into the arms of lesbian vampire Countess Nadine Carody (Soledad Miranda). In both *Planet of Blood* (1966) and *Lifeforce* (1985), human beings bring vampires back to earth from outer space.

A characteristic of vampire movies thus is an unusual emphasis on geographic and often transnational mobility. 'Quite simply', as Davies puts it, 'vampires travel a good deal' (2008: 396). Vampire movies are always about *motion*. Either the vampire or the protagonists (or the vampire as protagonist in a film such as *Interview With the Vampire*) are arriving from or going to someplace else. This perhaps is most evident in vampire films in which vampires or vampire hunters are constantly on the move. In *Vampire Circus* (1972), for example, vampires are part of an itinerant group of carnival workers, while in *Near Dark* (1987), a 'family' of vampires makes the rounds in a beat-up van. In contrast, in *Captain Kronos – Vampire Hunter* (1974), *John Carpenter's Vampires* (1998) and *The Forsaken* (2001), it is the vampire hunters who make the rounds, traveling from place to place and rooting out vampiric evil as they go.

In Stacey Abbott's estimation, this emphasis on movement is part of the essential modernity of Bram Stoker's *Dracula* and of cinematic vampires in general. The vampire is a force of movement and change, in a constant state of 'disintegration and renewal' (2007: 5). This constant movement of the vampire forces a reconceptualisation – or what philosophers Gilles Deleuze and Félix Guattari might refer to as a deterritorialisation – of both space and time as the vampire transcends the limitations of its own body, communicates psychically across distances and defies linear temporality.

The vampire inhabits what we may wish to think of as 'vampire space' – a smooth space in which thought overcomes distance and movement is unimpeded by either material obstacles or national boundaries. Those who pursue the vampire are at a distinct disadvantage as they must have recourse to all manner of conventional transportation and are subject to the laws of time and physics, as well as to those imposed by governments. Vampiric motion, in keeping with the vampire in general, is reflective both of dread and desire – anxiety over the unstability of a modern world 'perpetually in the throes of massive change' (Abbott 2007: 5), as well as the desire to transcend the limitations of time and place and become something other.

– Principle 4: The cinematic vampire is an overdetermined body condensing what a culture considers 'other'

Vampires, as we shall see, resist any all-encompassing one-to-one metaphoric interpretation. It is just too simple and reductive to say that the vampire is the metaphorical embodiment of devouring female sexuality or alternative configurations of sexual desire or of capitalist exploitation or of viral contagion or of xenophobia. Rather, the cinematic vampire is invariably an overdetermined body that condenses a constellation of culturally specific anxieties and desires into one super-saturated form. Any given vampire may clearly lend itself to one particular interpretive possibility, but – as with any text – is never exhausted by a single interpretation. Interpretation of Stoker's *Dracula* has become a sort of cottage industry precisely because the text supports so many different approaches and interpretations. This is what Judith Halberstam expresses in *Skin Shows: Gothic Horror and the Technology of Monsters* when she characterises his Dracula as a 'technology of monstrosity' (1995: 88), a 'composite of otherness' (1995: 90) that 'transform[s] the fragments of otherness into one body' (1995: 92) – one body that 'is not female, not Jewish, not homosexual, but ... bears the marks of the constructions of femininity, race, and sexuality' (1995: 92). Auerbach says more or less the same thing when she comments that Stoker's *Dracula* is a 'compendium of *fin-de-siècle* phobias' (1995: 7). As I will discuss in the pages that follow, what makes the vampire so potent is that it is a concatenation of sexual, racial and technological anxieties and longings – a sort of Rorschach ink blot of culturally specific dread and desire.

– Principle 5: The cinematic vampire is always about technology

>> Corollary 5.1: Vampire films are always about defining the vampire, which is a necessary preliminary to destroying the vampire
>> Corollary 5.2: Vampires are always cyborgs
>> Corollary 5.3: Vampire films are always about the cinema itself

Vampire movies, like monster movies in general, are always about defini-tion. People start sickening and dying, the vampire is first suspected and then confronted, and sooner or later the inevitable question gets posed: 'Good God, *what is it*?' The answer to this question – usually provided in the vampire cinema by a Van Helsing who is an expert on occult matters but in some cases provided by a book of arcane lore – is then a necessary pre-liminary to developing a strategy of response to the vampire's predations. What the protagonists conclude about the nature of the vampire, however – whether it is 'natural' or 'supernatural', whether it functions in accord-ance with scientific laws as we know them or outside of those laws – has important ramifications not only for deciding how to combat the vampire but for understanding how the represented cinematic world works.

The quest to understand the nature of the vampire and to develop an epistemological framework that encompasses it, which then allows one to determine how to fight the vampire, is a conscious theme that occurs in cinema as early as *Nosferatu* and becomes an increasing preoccupation of twentieth- and now twenty-first-century film. In keeping with Tzetvan Todorov's ruminations on the genre of the fantastic in general in *The Fantastic* (1973), there are two potential answers to the question of the vam-pire's nature: either the vampire is a naturally existing creature that can be assimilated into our understanding of how the world works (what Todorov refers to as the 'fantastic-uncanny') or the vampire violates our conceptual frameworks necessitating a revision of our understanding of the world (the 'fantastic-marvelous'). The vampire is either possible or impossible; when it is the latter, we need to rethink possibility itself.

A somewhat more nuanced categorical schema, however, is needed here to think about the vampire's relationship to nature and possibility: the vampire can be a 'naturally' occurring species like a vampire bat or Venus Flytrap acting in accordance with its nature; alternatively, the vampire can be an 'unnatural' human being – that is, a neurotic, psychotic or 'infected' individual whose behaviour is not in accordance with 'normal' human desires and behaviour, but whose behaviour does not violate the laws of nature as we know them; finally, the vampire can be 'supernatural', a creature whose actions and behaviour are outside of or transcend the laws of nature as we know them and whose existence necessitates a revision of those laws. We can think of these possibilities as the three branches of the vampire family tree: the *natural* vampire (separate species or a result of some natural process), the *unnatural* vampiric psychopath or viral host, and the *supernatural* vampire monster.

Once conclusions have been drawn about the nature of the vampire, the protagonists in vampire movies proceed to determining how to combat it. In general, natural and unnatural vampires are combated using conventional technological means. Bats and leeches and psychopaths can be captured and killed and courses of treatment can be developed for viruses. Supernatural vampires require a different approach, different tools and a different knowledge base. Rather than having recourse to modern science and weaponry, one combats the supernatural vampire, as exemplified in films including *The Lost Boys*, *Fright Night* and *'Salem's Lot* (1979), by drawing upon the repository of vampire knowledge constituted by folklore, literature and the cinematic tradition. The vampire is then tracked, thwarted and killed by using the set of tools specified in the tradition – garlic, stakes, sunlight, holy water, and so forth. (As I will discuss in Chapter Two, more recent vampire movies, such as the *Blade* and *Underworld* series, as well as *The Breed* (2001) and *Van Helsing* (2004), have interestingly combined modern technology with literary and folkloric weapons, leading to various forms of light grenades, silver-bullet machineguns and vampire-killing viruses.)

Ultimately, whether vampirism is caused by viral contagion or demonic agency, and whether the antidote is an inoculation or holy water, the determination of what the vampire is and how to deal with it leads to a consid-eration and sometimes revision of existing epistemological paradigms and to an engagement with technology. The vampire thus, in an even more specific way than is suggested by Allucquère Rosanne Stone in her consideration of Anne Rice's vampire Lestat (1995: 178–80), is always a sort of cyborg, defined in relation to and, in many cases, produced by particular technologies of detection, determination and destruction. Vampire films thereby function as referendums on the inadequacies, perils and promises of modern science and technology.

There is another sense though in which the vampire is a product of and in some cases a conscious meditation on the human relationship to technology – and here we must think about the vampire as a product of cinema, as a creation of light and shadow projected onto a blank screen in a darkened room. The cinematic vampire is clearly the product of constantly evolving cinema technology: of make-up, special effects, and all the 'magic' of movie making from sound and colour to computer-generated imagery (CGI). Our imagining of vampires in large measure has been influenced by their representations on screen. As I will argue in Chapter Two, however, the cinema and the vampire need to be considered as twins, born at the same time and mutually inflecting the imagining of each other. So in the same way that the vampire is a cinematic creation, the cinema will be discussed as a vampiric creation.

– Principle 6: The vampire film genre does not exist

›› Corollary 6.1: The vampire film tradition is defined by generic hybridity
›› Corollary 6.2: Vampire films are inevitably intertextual

It is tempting to think of vampire films as constituting either a sub-genre of the horror film or as a genre unto themselves. Auerbach, however, rightly asserts that 'There is no such creature as "The Vampire"; there are only vampires' (1995: 15). The number and diversity of vampire films prevents any sort of simplistic categorisation. What the natural/unnatural/supernatural tri-partite classificatory schema observed above foregrounds is in fact the generic hybridity of the vampire film that will be emphasised in this book's concluding chapter. Depending upon whether the vampire is figured as natural, unnatural or supernatural, the vampire film will exist somewhere along a continuum ranging from science fiction horror to fantasy horror. The vampire as naturally existing species combines horror with science fiction – it extrapolates from what is to what could be without violating the laws of nature as we know them. 'Natural' vampires can include vampires from outer space as well as terrestrial humanoid vampires and creatures such as vampire bats and leeches acting in accordance with their nature, as long as their actions are also in accordance with natural laws (i.e. that are not supernatural creatures, but simply other species that live among us). 'Unnatural' vampires can similarly contain science fictive elements such as when the vampire is created through genetic mutation or infection, as in David Cronenberg's *Rabid* (1977) or all the films spawned by Richard Matheson's novel *I Am Legend*, including the 2007 film version of the same name starring Will Smith. And when the vampire is a supernatural creature, a monster that defies the laws of physics and has 'magical' powers, we generally have fantasy horror.

But even this classificatory schema is insufficient because of the numerous attempts to introduce vampires into other cinematic traditions beyond horror, fantasy and science fiction. Thus one can point to the vampire western (*Curse of the Undead* (1959); *Billy the Kid vs. Dracula* (1966); *BloodRayne II: Deliverance* (2007); *Near Dark*), the vampire action film (the *Blade* films (1998, 2002, 2004); the *Underworld* films (2003, 2006, 2009); *Van Helsing*), the vampire comedy (*Love at First Bite*; *Dracula: Dead and Loving It* (1995)), even the vampire gangster film (*Vampires in Havana* (1985); *Innocent Blood* (1992)). And then there are films like *The Breed* (to be discussed in Chapter Three) that combine elements from several generic categories into a kind of generic vampire bricolage. There are art-house vampire films, summer vampire blockbusters, campy 'B' vampire productions, underground vampire cult films – and real head-scratchers like *Jesus Christ Vampire Hunter* (2001) or the especially quirly *Bubba Ho-tep* (2002). Indeed, the only vampire constant is that the vampire film must include an entity of some kind that drains others – generally of blood but sometimes of life-force or energy.

The sheer number and diversity of vampire films makes it impossible to talk about any kind of coherent 'vampire film genre'. Indeed, as will be discussed in this book's concluding chapter, a fundamental characteristic of the vampire film tradition has been its tendency to morph and colonise other genres – which helps explain the staying power of the vampire cinema. Like the vampire itself, the vampire cinema continually transforms itself and seeks out new victims to vamp.

That said, it also needs to be acknowledged that each innovation in cinematic vampire representation and excursion outward into uncharted generic or thematic terrain is accompanied by a backwards glance and knowing wink. At the centre of the vampire cinema solar system is Bram Stoker's *Dracula*, the vampire Ur-text that exerts a powerful gravitational attraction and around which all vampire texts – literary, cinematic and otherwise – necessarily orbit. All representations of vampires inevitably are measured against the defining image offered by Bram Stoker and then concretised by Bela Lugosi. In other words, we are only able to recognise what is original in a vampire film by comparing it to the familiar representation derived from this source novel – and on some level virtually every vampire film suffers from this anxiety of influence. In many cases, such as *Blade: Trinity* or *Dracula 2000* (which imaginatively goes so far as to recast Dracula as Judas himself), films explicitly contrast their imagining of the vampire with Stoker's, pointing out what is 'true' and what is not. The audience, however, is presumed in every case to know the 'essential' characteristics of the vampire and to be able to distinguish faithfulness to established convention from innovation.

– Principle 7: We are all vampire textual nomads

What the last point above makes clear is that, borrowing from Henry Jenkins' concept of 'textual nomadism' famously introduced in *Textual Poachers* (1992), we are all 'vampire textual nomads'. We cannot just watch a single vampire movie; instead, we are always watching many vampire movies simultaneously, comparing the new representation with the old, recognising the extent to which the new portrayal conforms to or diverges from the sedimented conventions of the vampire cinema and looking for the seemingly inevitable winks to the audience at the moments that a new vampire film metatextually acknowledges itself as participating in and revising an established tradition. Among the questions that we come prepared to ask are: Is the vampire natural or supernatural? Is it affected by religious iconography or not? Is the vampire attractive or repulsive? Can he or she transform? Or Fly? And is the vampire hunter a serious male professional? A teenage boy? A perky blonde cheerleader? This process of mental comparison is, of course, most apparent with each new representation of Dracula. One cannot help but compare Gerard Butler in *Dracula 2000* to Gary Oldman in *Bram Stoker's Dracula* (1992) to Frank Langella in *Dracula* (1979) to Christopher Lee in his many portrayals of The Count to Bela Lugosi, and so forth. We are thus all vampire nomads; we range freely among a profusion of vampire texts, considering one in light of our knowledge of and experiences of others.

Indeed, vampires have so thoroughly colonised the Western cultural imaginary that one need not actually have read Bram Stoker's *Dracula* or seen even a single vampire movie to know the vampire basics – they drink blood, come out only at night, can transform, are destroyed with a stake, and so forth. There are at this point no vampire virgins – at least none over the age of ten with access to popular culture in some way, shape or form. We are all bitten from the moment we see 'Count von Count' on *Sesame Street* or Count Chocula on a cereal box or experience our first Halloween – and it is this observation that forms the core of this book. In the course of James Twitchell's analysis of literary vampires, he observes that 'Any twelve-year-old schoolboy can describe the vampire, and that of course is precisely why it is so important' (1985: 110). Vampires are so ubiquitous, so much a part of our lives, that the relative absence of critical attention to the thousands of vampires movies in existence is almost suspicious. What is it we are afraid to find there?

Clearly, the vampire strikes a chord in contemporary popular culture. This book looks at the vampire tradition in cinema and considers why the cinematic vampire is so ubiquitous and so compelling. The vampire, I conclude, is a sort of ready-made metaphoric vehicle waiting for its tenor. Its potency, however, derives from its intrinsic connections to sex, science and social constructions of difference. The three chapters that follow take as their organising premises three of the principles presented above: the vampire film is always about sex, always about technology and always about cultural 'otherness'. The other principles will be developed along the way and this book concludes with a fuller consideration of the ways in which the vampire cinema defies generic categorisation. The sheer volume of vampire films in existence obviously limits me to discussing only a small percentage of them and I'm tempted to add as a final Principle here that this book will inevitably omit attention to what the reader considers an essential film – that, too, is part of being a vampire textual nomad. Discussion of one vampire film inevitably calls to mind others and since the vampire always escapes, there is no way finally to stake him in place – but it sure is fun trying.

1 VAMPIRE SEX

> It's not easy to put your finger on what's appealing about zombies. Vampires you can understand. They're good-looking and sophisticated and well dressed. They're immortal. Some of them have castles. You can imagine wanting to be a vampire or at least wanting to sleep with one. Nobody wants to sleep with zombies.
>
> – Lev Grossman (2009)

As this quotation from *Time Magazine* staff writer Lev Grossman makes clear in an April 2009 column on zombies, most movie monsters have very selective sexual appeal. Zombies are lousy kissers with terrible personal hygiene (but, Grossman fails to note, at least they are sincere when they tell you they like you for your brains!). Mummies might attract fans of *The English Patient* (1996), but sand in the sheets can be unpleasant and they're poor conversationalists at best. The werewolf's closeted lifestyle quickly becomes tiresome (as do all the inevitable 'there wolf' jokes). And blobs are poor sharers. But vampires, plain and simple, are *sexy* and have been throughout the history of cinema.

The limited (but rapidly growing) scholarly literature on cinematic vampires emphasises that, more so than any other movie monster, vampires are inextricably interconnected with the idea of sex. This was psychoanalyst Ernest Jones's conclusion in his 1931 study *On the Nightmare* when he links the vampire to folkloric beliefs in the incubus and succubus – demons or evil spirits that engage in sexual congress with the living. Combining Rosemary Jackson's contention that 'the vampire myth is perhaps the highest symbolic representation of eroticism' (1981: 120) with Robin Wood's influential assertion that 'monsters' in general give shape to repressed sexual energies (1985), Richard Dyer concludes that vampirism in both film and literature 'evoke[s] the thrill of forbidden sexuality' (1988: 64). Focusing on the Hammer Studios vampire films of the 1970s, Ken Gelder maintains that Hammer's lesbian vampires cemented the association between vampirism and 'perverse' sexual behaviour (1994: 98). And David Pirie in his excellent survey of vampire movies concisely asserts that 'there has never been any question that the primary appeal of the films lay in their latent erotic content' (1977: 6).

In my opinion, Dyer, Gelder and Pirie are exactly right when they connect cinematic vampirism to erotic titillation, but they are also curiously circumspect. While it is the premise of this book that vampire films inevitably engage on varying levels with certain key cultural concerns and social issues – our relationship to technology and constructions of 'otherness' among them – the cinematic vampire first and foremost must be recognised as a sexual entity. Indeed, 'latent' seems exactly the *wrong* word to describe the overt eroticism associated with Theda Bara's seduction of 'the fool' in *A Fool There Was* (1915), Christopher Lee's animalistic hunger for Lucy in her bedroom in *Horror of Dracula* (1958) or Catherine Deneuve and Susan Sarandon's role in the sheets in *The Hunger* (1983)! My argument here is that, more so than any other cinematic category or genre apart from pornography itself, vampire movies (which often border on and occasionally cross into porn; witness *Spermula* (1976), *Buffy the Vampire Layer* (2002), *Ejacula* (2008), and so forth) deal explicitly in sexual desire – the vampire is the cinema's most potent instanciation of sexual excess and what I will term 'hyperbolic gender'. Not only can you image 'wanting to sleep with one' (Grossman), my argument is that cinema has so thoroughly sexualised the vampire that it is next to impossible *not* to imagine the vampire sleeping with – or at least nibbling erotically on – someone.

The vampire in both literature and film embodies transgressive, tabooed sexuality – hypnotic, overwhelming, selfish and destructive. The vampiric body, itself frequently represented as fluid and transformative, courses with polymorphously perverse sexual energy that refuses to be channeled into respectable heterosexual monogamy. The vampiric attack conventionally involves an intimate physical encounter outside of marriage and the exchange of bodily fluids – the vampire's 'kiss' – frequently at night in the private space of the bedroom. (And, as Dyer notes, although you don't absolutely have to interpret the vampire's biting someone on the neck and sucking the blood as sexual, an awful lot suggests you should! (1988: 155)). Sexualised vampiric appetite – whether heterosexual, homosexual or bisexual in orientation – always exceeds and defies cultural mores. The vampire dominates its victim and does not just seek to penetrate, but to absorb, literally to drain the life away from his or her partner. As such, the vampire clearly can be considered a manifestation of the Freudian Id – as the pleasure principle run amuck. (From this perspective, the vampire hunters of course then represent the Super-Ego attempting to put a halt to the Id's destructive rampage. The body of the victim, which literally mediates contending tabooed and repressive forces, is cast in the role of Ego.) In short, vampirism, according to Dyer, is the alternative to following society's restrictive sexual mandates, 'dreaded and desired in equal measure' (1988: 64).

The overriding premise of this chapter is that it is next to impossible to think the cinematic vampire without thinking sex – part (if not most) of the appeal of the vampire genre is its titillating engagement with transgressive sexual desires and taboos. And the implications of this are important because vampire movies do not just reflect societal mores through their representations of eroticism; they implicitly (and sometimes explicitly) code specific behaviours as acceptable and unacceptable, thus reifying and reproducing sexual stereotypes and cultural understandings of what constitutes acceptable and unacceptable sexual behaviour, even as they trouble those same social expectations by raising questions – usually implicitly but sometimes even explicitly – about their presumed naturalness. But whether repressive or subversive, queer vampire movies (movies featuring excessively masculine or feminine vampires, bisexual or homosexual vampires, vampires that get off on drinking blood – vampires that foreground in various ways the arbitrariness, 'unnaturalness' and/or cultural constructedness of gender and sexual codes) need to be considered as a form of discourse about sexuality. They talk about sex endlessly and in so many ways. They give shape to inchoate desire even as they then carefully categorise sexual proclivities as acceptable and unacceptable. This ultimately is the dual polarity of the vampire film – and, I would add, of film in general: interpellation into the world of cinema produces spectators both as desiring subjects and subjects subject to the law. Vampire films, I suggest, offer the contradictory command 'Here's what you shouldn't think about, so think about it!'

Below, I will consider representations of the vampire as embodying tabooed, excessive and 'perverse' sexuality. Since sex and the cinematic vampire is the topic that has received the most attention in the academic literature, I will attempt to note what has already been said while attending primarily to a variety of movies that have been (fairly or not) ignored by scholars up to this point. I will begin by considering what I will call the 'hyperbolic gender' of the vampire – the vampire as sexually irresistible seducer who pushes masculinity or femininity into the realm of monstrosity, thereby foregrounding the constructedness of gender itself. Here I will rapidly cover the history of vampire movies by attending both to the earliest and one of the most recent movies to be considered in this study, *A Fool There Was* from 1915 and *Twilight* released in 2008. I will then turn my attention to the topic that has received the most attention from academics – the vampire and homosexuality. While giving some attention to the films that have received the most scrutiny in this category – mainly *Dracula's Daughter* (1936) – I will focus in more depth on a trio of lesbian-themed vampire movies all released in 1971: Jesús Franco's cult classic, *Vampyros Lesbos*; Jean Rollin's lushly erotic *Requiem for a Vampire*; and the sublime Belgian production, *Daughters of Darkness*. I will round things out by considering *Interview With the Vampire* because, in keeping with Anne Rice's novel, it highlights in such a visible way what has been kept tightly under wraps even in the vampire genre – male homoeroticism. My conclusion is that vampire movies constitute an explicit, pervasive and conflicted cinematic discourse concerning sexuality that both reconfirms and troubles conventional sexual norms.

Strange Attractors 1: The Vamp

While ideas about vampires and cinema are both culturally specific and dynamic, one constant that stretches back to the earliest days of cinema is the connections between vampires, liberated libido and hyperbolic gender. Another way to put this is that cinematic vampires teach us what it means to be an acceptably sexual man or woman by showing us what it means to be a 'perversely' sexual monster. In film's first decades, however, the vampire was not a charismatic or hypnotic male seducer, not a suave Bela Lugosi or commanding Christopher Lee stealing our women and turning them into monsters by instilling in them or – more provocatively – *awakening* in them their slumbering sexuality, but instead a predatory female, the *belle dame sans merci*, who contravened the laws of nature by actively controlling and debilitating men. This is to say that the first cinematic vampires were vamps: women who appropriated the masculine agency utilised in seduction, who refused to restrict their sexuality to procreative heterosexual monogamy sanctioned by marriage, and who 'unmanned' their victims by rendering them passive and dependent – women, in short, who acted like men and who transformed men into characters coded as feminine. David Pirie comments that early films used the word 'vampire' 'simply as an innocuous alternative for *femme fatale* or vamp' (1977: 134) and Andrea Weiss in her analysis of lesbians in film concurs, noting that in the early days of cinema, the word 'vampire' connoted 'vamp' – a 'beautiful woman whose sexual desire, if fulfilled, would drain the life blood of man' (1993: 96). Weiss goes on to note that cinema's first decade of existence featured 'at least forty films about this mortal female vampire, whom men could find sexually enticing while women could fantasize female empowerment' (1993: 97).

Pirie and Weiss are undeniably right here to note the ubiquity of the vamp in early cinema, but I think the logic needs a slight adjustment. Putting aside the fact that it is hard to see how using the word 'vampire' to refer to a 'predatory' woman is 'innocuous', the timeline is slightly askew. It is not that early films were using the word 'vampire' in place of the existing word 'vamp' – 'vamp' as an abbreviation for 'vampire' connoting a woman who intentionally attracts and exploits men was a relatively new coinage in the 1910s (the OED traces it to 1911). Rather, I think it is more accurate to say that early cinema *invented* the vamp. Literary history of course is filled with dark female temptresses; however, the vamp as female sexual vampire is arguably a cinematic creation that emerged during the first decade of cinema, and no one had more to do with cementing the association between vampirism and hyperbolic female sexuality than 'the screen's original vamp' Theda Bara (see Genini 1996: 21–6).

Born Theodosia Goodman, the daughter of a Jewish tailor in Cincinnati, Bara starred in more than forty films between 1914 and 1926, is often regarded as cinema's first true sex symbol and, as noted above, is considered the original screen 'vamp'. In order to capitalise on her 'exotic' looks and to create an air of mystery around her, she famously was photographed in Oriental-themed attire and a fictional biography was invented for her in which she was the Egyptian-born daughter of a French actress and an Italian sculptor who had spent her early years in the Sahara Desert under the shadow of the Sphinx before moving to France to become a stage actress. Although sometimes referred to as the 'Serpent of the Nile' (she played Cleopatra in the eponymous 1917 production), her *femme fatal* roles – including the role of a character referred to only as 'The Vampire' in *A Fool There Was* – lead to her also being nicknamed 'The Vamp'. At the height of her popularity, Bara was making $4,000 per week for her film performances and ranked behind only silent screen stars Charlie Chaplin and Mary Pickford in popularity (again, see Genini 1996).

According to Ronald Genini, *A Fool There Was* essentially introduced the term 'vamp' (both as a noun *and* as a verb) to the American pop culture vocabulary. While this is a difficult claim to substantiate, the movie – which takes as its inspiration and occasionally quotes from Rudyard Kipling's 1897 poem 'The Vampire', which chronicles the downfall of a man seduced by a woman oblivious to or unconcerned about the consequences of her actions – undeniably cements the association between vampirism and destructive female sexuality. In the film, although she has a lover at the start (Reginald

A Fool There Was: 'The Vampire' kisses her fool

Parmalee, played by actor Victor Benoit) who acts like a lap-dog living off the scraps of her affection, The Vampire quickly sets her sights on lawyer John Schuyler (Edward José), who has been identified in the newspaper as having been named 'Special Representative of the U.S. Government to England' by the Secretary of State and who is about to embark on a trans-Atlantic journey *sans* wife and golden-haired daughter. The Vampire makes arrangements to join Schuyler aboard ship and, as she steps out of her motor coach at the docks, she is confronted by a clearly destitute former lover who calls her a 'hell cat' before being hauled off at her request by the police. Then, as the ship is preparing to embark, she is threatened on deck by her current lover, Parmalee, whom she is abandoning and who brandishes a gun at her. Her response is simply to laugh in his face, prompting him to commit suicide. In a particularly ghoulish gesture, the cleaned-off deck has barely had the chance to dry when she has her deck chair placed on the spot of her ex-lover's suicide and directs that the chair of her next victim, Schuyler, be put next to hers.

By the time the ship reaches its destination, the seduction is a *fait accompli* and Schuyler is under her spell; indeed, the seduction, which apart from The Vampire's initial machinations before the ship embarks is never shown, is made to seem both effortless and magical. After the ship sets sail, when next we see Schuyler it is two months later and he is seated on the ground leaning against The Vampire who lounges in a divan in a tropical Italian setting. Schuyler appears drugged; fed cordials by The Vampire, he is unable to rise. He has abandoned both political post and his wife and daughter. Other Americans visiting the same locale, appalled by his behaviour, refuse to stay in the same hotel and his exploits find their way into 'The Town Tattler' section of a New York newspaper that reports that 'A certain millionaire reformer, who was sent abroad as a special ambassadorial envoy some months ago, has fatuously fallen under the spell of a certain notorious woman of the vampire species, not wholly unconnected with the dramatic suicide of young Reginald Parmalee aboard the Cunarder "Gigantic" the day it sailed...'.

After being dismissed from his post for naughty behaviour, we next see a visibly aged Schuyler and The Vampire back in the United States where they are installed in Schuyler's urban townhouse. Schuyler's hair has gone completely grey, he has dark circles under his eyes, and he appears pallid, weak and off-balance. In one of the film's most interesting sequences,

Schuyler's wife and child pull alongside Schuyler and The Vampire's motor coach on a busy road and his daughter calls plaintively, 'Papa, dear, I want you!' Back at the townhouse, The Vampire berates the haggard and distraught Schuyler, chastising him, 'Why did you act afraid and ashamed? You should have bowed and smiled, as I did.' She then pours him a drink – this is the beginning of the end for Schuyler.

The rest of the film chronicles Schuyler's rapid deterioration and his subsequent abandonment by The Vampire. As Schuyler drinks more and more, he neglects both his business affairs and his appearance. Six months pass and when we see Schuyler next, he is so drunk he can barely stand. His servants have abandoned him and The Vampire has taken up with another man. Nevertheless, each time an attempt is made to rescue Schuyler and return him to his wife – first by his friend and secretary, second by his wife and child – The Vampire returns and exerts her irresistible will upon his; even though she no longer wants him, she refuses to allow anyone else to claim him. In the film's penultimate scene, the abandoned Schuyler crawls down a dark staircase in his empty townhouse, at one point peering and reaching through gaps in the banister railing as if through prison bars, and continues across his parlour where, in the midst of smashing a bottle, he is stricken and collapses. Quoting from the Kipling poem, the intertitle reads 'Some of him lived, but the most of him died'. Then we see The Vampire hovering over Schuyler's prostrate body, smiling and dropping flower petals on his face. The final intertitle, again quoting from the Kipling poem, reads '(Even as you and I.)' and then the camera iris closes, fading out on The Vampire hovering ghoulishly over Schuyler.

The Vampire in *A Fool There Was* is not literally a vampire in the sense of being 'undead'. Nonetheless, she constitutes the uncanny irruption of powerful, almost supernatural forces into the mundane life-world of her victims. She is a primal force of unleashed sexuality that holds her lovers in thrall and she embodies the essence of the vampire as a creature that lives off the life force of others. While she does not drink Schuyler's blood, she does literally drain his vitality – at the start, he is depicted as healthy and only greying about the temples; at the end, he is decrepit and his hair has turned entirely grey. And her seductive, hypnotic power clearly anticipates the mesmeric gaze of subsequent cinematic vampire representations.

Indeed, what is most uncanny about The Vampire – in keeping with cinematic vampires in general – is that, feeding off the life force of her victims, she is in fact *more alive* than the living around her. In concluding by quoting Kipling's poem, 'The Vampire', with the lines, 'So some of him lived but the most of him died – (Even as you or I!)', the import of the 'even as you or I' here is that we, the living, are always already partly – even mostly – dead. We are all in various ways 'fools' that fail to live our lives to the fullest. Kipling here arguably channels the psychoanalytic theorising of Jacques Lacan *avant la lettre* and, indeed, the representation of The Vampire in *A Fool There Was* corresponds exactly to Slavoj Žižek's Lacanian assertion that the paradox of the living dead is that they are 'far more alive' than the living (2002: 221). This is the irony that lurks beneath Ellis Hanson's comment that 'The vampire is always more appealing and exciting than the men and women who hunt it' (1999: 191). The Vampire in *A Fool There Was*, without name, family or social obligation, lives for pleasure alone. She is a figure of excessive – and thus threatening – enjoyment, an uncanny surplus that transgresses social expectations and highlights the precariousness of gender codes.

Weiss suggests that The Vampire in *A Fool There Was* is sexually enticing to heterosexual men and offers to women a model of female empowerment. This may be, yet the clear message of the film is that women such as The Vampire are bad news. Yes, The Vampire is dark, mysterious and enticingly sexual; but she is also sadistic, selfish and hedonistic – in a word, evil. She is a drug more powerful than the alcohol to which Schuyler turns for forgetfulness and when it no longer amuses her to feed his habit, she simply abandons him. All of this is to say that, in *A Fool There Was*, The Vampire (every bit as much as Countess Irina von Karstein in Jesús Franco's *Female Vampire* (1973) who literalises the metaphor of draining life force through sex by surviving on oral sex that kills her victims) embodies cultural anxieties about female sexuality. It thus is not difficult to see *A Fool There Was* – and the some forty other films of the 1910s and 1920s that feature predatory female vamps – as manifesting a conservative backlash against the 'New Woman' of the 1890s and feminist agitation in the first decades of the twentieth century.

Perhaps most interesting about *A Fool There Was* is that there is no final redemption for Schuyler or punishment for The Vampire. Schuyler does not shake off The Vampire's baleful influence and re-embrace his wife and child, nor does The Vampire experience contrition or have visited upon her the righteous indignation of the wronged wife; instead, The Vampire's victory is complete. Her grip on Schuyler's being is so iron-clad that not even the pathetic pleadings of his angelic daughter can shake it loose. The message seems to be that The Vampire is still out there, searching for her next victim. Men, therefore, should arm themselves as best they can against the predatory vamps of the world by devoting themselves to family, country, God and industry. And women, if they wish to retain the respect of the world at large, must keep their sexuality under wraps – confined to the marital bed – and remain (to borrow from Barbara Welter's 1985 analysis of the nineteenth-century 'Cult of True Womanhood') pious, pure, domestic and subservient.

Strange Attractors 2: More Manly Than Man

If the female vampire usurps the masculine privilege of agency and is coded as unnatural by virtue of her predatory sexuality, the male vampire has increasingly in twentieth- and now twenty-first-century cinema been coded as hyper-masculine: powerful, attractive, sexual and courageous. While there have been occasional deviations from the formula in which the vampire is physically hideous from the start – call them members of the Nosferatu clan (notably the vampire Barlow in the 1979 TV-miniseries adaptation of Stephen King's *'Salem's Lot* who is a clear descendent of Max Schreck's Count Orlok in *Nosferatu*) – for the most part the male vampire has been represented as masculine to the point of gender parody. The irony of the modern vampire is that he is more manly than man – and, in being such, reveals both the contingency and impossibility of masculinity.

Any number of cinematic texts come to mind when considering the hyper-masculinity of the cinematic vampire (one thinks not only of Bela Lugosi and Christopher Lee, but also of Frank Langella in *Dracula*; Wesley Snipes in *Blade*; Tom Cruise, Brad Pitt, and Antonio Banderas in *Interview With the Vampire*; Gary Oldman in *Bram Stoker's Dracula*, Kiefer Sutherland in *The Lost Boys*, and so on) but I wish to focus here on *Twilight* because it takes the idea of the male vampire as (literal) *übermensch* further than any cinematic text so far. In *Twilight*, vampire Edward Cullen (Robert Pattinson) is ironically the perfect contemporary man by virtue of not being human. Not only is he considered especially alluring (one is tempted to say toothsome!) by the student population of the Forks, Washington state high school – even without the opportunity to see how his skin shimmers in sunlight – but in his courtship of Bella (Kristen Stewart), he is revealed as super strong, super fast and sensitive enough to take his date to the top of a tall tree to enjoy a sublime scenic vista. As a vampire, Edward is, baring dismemberment and incineration, immortal and, as if that weren't enough, he possesses the power to read minds – all except for protagonist Bella's. Edward's only apparent flaw is his taste for blood, but even this is mitigated by his 'vampire vegetarian' lifestyle – he and his 'family' restrict their consumption to animal blood. No wonder the Internet is rife with assertions and lamentations that Stephenie Meyer's *Twilight* series creates unrealistic expectations of men!

In short, Edward is much more angel than monster, his shimmering skin suggestive of a displaced halo. He possesses all the attractions of Lestat and Louis in *Interview With the Vampire* without Lestat's sadism and Louis' angst. His star-crossed 'forbidden love' romance with Bella combines the Cinderella fairytale of the girl from the wrong side of the tracks landing a prince with the super-hero narrative – Bella must keep Edward's 'real identity' under wraps. In fact, the minor annoyance of being stalked by rival vampires aside, Bella's romance with Edward offers her everything her heart might desire: a sexy, sensitive boyfriend who can barely control his lust for her; affluence and social status; a ready-made family; the bond created by a shared secret; a world of marvels generally denied to the rank and file of humanity; and the tantalising possibility of immortality. What mortal man could compete with that?

Edward as vampire hero is the apotheosis of one model of hyperbolic modern masculinity. He does not transgress gender expectations in the way that The Vampire does in *A Fool There Was*; rather, he is their perfection. The result, however, is strangely similar. The Vampire's libidinous violation of cultural codes of femininity reveals what one might refer to as the 'myth' of femininity – myth here understood in the sense developed by Roland Barthes in his *Mythologies* (1972) as the naturalisation of something historical and contingent. The Vampire shows us that to be a woman means to act in accordance with a particular set of cultural expectations that are arguably not 'natural' at all but cultural – most notable among them is the idea that women should lack sexual desire. Similarly, Edward as masculine perfection show us – to do a little twist on Lacan – that The Man does not exist; that is, Edward shows us first that ideas of what it means to be a man are a product of converging lines of social and historical forces and second that no actual man can fulfil all cultural expectations completely.

The *übermensch* – the man who does not lack in some respect – is by necessity a monster. Here we return again to that ironic proposition that what both attracts and repels about the vampire is her or his excessiveness – the vampire as 'surplus in an otherwise coherent system of identification' (Gelder 1994: 52 (glossing Žižek)).

Lesbian Vampires (Or, 'What Vampire Porn Are You Watching Today?')

While preparing to write this book, I spent a summer watching vampire movies just about every day (there are worse ways to spend a summer!). And inevitably my wife would choose to enter the room at precisely the moment that voluptuous naked female bodies filled the screen, prompting the question (with, to her credit, only a slight note of exasperation in her voice), 'What vampire porn are you watching today?' In retrospect, I've come to appreciate that her quip offers a concise rendering of the central claim of this chapter: that is, that it is very, very difficult – if not impossible – to think the cinematic vampire without thinking sex. Vampire films, particularly those made during the boom in vampire movies at the height of 'porn chic' in the 1970s, are all about bodies (often sexy ones) interacting with other bodies (also sexy ones) in intimate ways – and often without much clothing on to get in the way. Vampire movies, always on some level about sex, thus constitute a discourse of sexuality that participates in shaping cultural attitudes toward gender and sexuality.

Although vampire sex takes a variety of forms – from the decorously heterosexual to the polymorphously perverse – my argument is that vampires are nonetheless inevitably 'queer'; by recklessly transgressing gender expectations and sexual mores they foreground the social constructedness of gender and sexual codes, as well as the hegemonic devices that attempt to naturalise those constructions. And nowhere is the queer sexuality of the vampire more readily apparent than in the prominence of the lesbian vampire character. Harry Benshoff observes that lesbian vampires can be found in 'each era of the English-language horror film' (1997: 191) and Carol Jenks proposes that lesbian vampires are so ubiquitous as to constitute 'an entire sub-genre of the horror film in itself' (1996: 22). Once one takes into consideration Weiss's assertion that 'outside of male pornography, the lesbian vampire is the most persistent lesbian image in the history of the cinema' (1993: 84), the significance of correlating vampirism and lesbianism in terms of shaping cultural attitudes becomes clear and raises a host of important questions about the production and consumption of such texts: What explains the frequency of lesbian vampires in cinema? What pleasures inhere in viewing such texts? If vampires are monsters who must be destroyed, does this mean that films featuring lesbian vampires are invariably and inevitably homophobic? Particularly given the interesting cultural shift we are witnessing in which vampires are being recast as heroes, is there a way in which the lesbian vampire can function to undermine, rather than reinforce, repressive attitudes toward 'alternative' sexualities?

Rather than speculate in the abstract, in order to engage these questions, I will first talk briefly about the film that has received the most commentary on the subject, *Dracula's Daughter* from 1936. I will then turn to a trio of films featuring lesbian vampires all released in 1971: Jesús Franco's *Vampyros Lesbos*, Jean Rollin's *Requiem for a Vampire* and Harold Kümel's *Daughters of Darkness*. Taken together, what these films demonstrate is not just the inextricable interconnection of vampirism and alternative configurations of erotic desire, but the conflicted nature of the vampire film – its reaffirmation of conventional sexual mores even as it invariably troubles sedimented understandings of 'human nature'.

Dracula's Daughter

Directed by Lambert Hillyer, who astonishingly directed over 160 films between 1917 and 1949, *Dracula's Daughter* has been the focus of intense scrutiny by film critics interested in recovering the traces of homosexual history embedded in cinema. The film centres on Countess Mayra Zaleska (Gloria Holden), who we learn is Dracula's daughter and shares his 'curse' – the necessity of existing on human blood. In an interesting twist, Countess Zaleska goes into therapy with psychologist Dr Jeffrey Garth (Otto Kruger) in the attempt to cure herself of her 'obsession'. Unfortunately, the therapy fails and the Countess, resigned to her vampirism, determines to make Dr Garth into her vampire companion. She lures him to her castle in Transylvania by kidnapping his assistant/love interest Janet (Marguerite Churchill) only to be shot through the heart by her jilted assistant Sandor (Irving Pichel) whom she had promised to make into a vampire.

According to Benshoff, Countess Zaleska who preys upon both men and women – but seems to relish attractive young women the most – and who seeks assistance from the psychologist Dr Garth in combating her deviant desire, is 'the most obviously "lesbian" monster movie of the classical period' (1997: 77) and lesbianism and vampirism blur together as 'evil forces that the heterosexual male must oppose' (1997: 195). The central scene supporting this assertion to which the critics turn is Zaleska's preying upon Lili (Nan Grey). Lured to Zaleska's Chelsea flat with the promise of food and shelter in exchange for posing as an artist's model, the undressed and vulnerable Lili becomes the object of Zaleska's uncontrollable (blood) lust. The camera focuses on the Countess as she advances upon Lili and, as Lili screams, the camera cuts away to an African mask hanging on the wall over the heads of the two women. In nuanced interpretations of this scene, critic Reynold Humphries reads the mask together with the veil that Zaleska draws over the lower-part of her face earlier in the film as together signifying 'the exotic, the erotic and the despotic, overdetermined by the necrophilic' (2000: 278), while Bonnie Burns emphasises what is *not* shown here: 'the possibility of a lesbian encounter' (1995: 205). Lesbianism remains beyond the limit of the visible; it is 'unrepresentable' (Jenks 1996: 23).

On the surface, *Dracula's Daughter* seems a straightforwardly homophobic film in which the correlation between lesbianism and vampirism participates in cementing into place 'the social construction of homosexuals as unnatural, predatory, plague-carrying killers' (Benshoff 1997: 14). Indeed, in a provocative twist, Zaleska's shameful secret, her 'unnatural' desire and self-hatred, is explicitly pathologised as she seeks psychological counselling in what Ellis Hanson considers a 'parody of a psychoanalytic case study' (1999: 197). Dr Garth's prescription, 'sympathetic treatment' consisting of 'will-power' and self-denial, as Benshoff points out, resembles many 'cures' for homosexuality (1997: 80). And in keeping with later lesbian vampire films, the central contest in the film centers on the control of women – Zaleska has kidnapped Janet and Garth must get her back. Perhaps most damningly, Zaleska, who is poised to vampirise Janet if Garth won't accede to her wishes (Hanson refers to Zaleska's hovering over Janet in this scene as 'what must be surely the longest kiss never filmed' (1999: 198)), is not staked by Garth or the police, but rather by another queer, her servant Sandor – 'a nay-saying bitchy queen' (Benshoff 1997: 78) – who desires to *become* a vampire. Vampires are queer, says the film, and queers are killers. With both Countess Zaleska and Sandor out of the way (Sandor is shot by the police) and thus the ominous specter of non-standard sexualities expunged from the film, there is nothing to prevent the obligatory heterosexual consummation of Garth and Janet's relationship. The queers are dead and heterosexuality rules the day.

But things are never quite that simple. First, as Benshoff mentions, 'normality' in the film is none too appealing as Dr Garth is 'an active misogynist' (1997: 80) who frankly doesn't seem to care about Janet all that much until Countess Zaleska makes off with her. Garth's concern arguably has more to do with the idea of possession than it does with sincere regard. Perhaps more importantly, Countess Zaleska (and perhaps to a lesser extent, Sandor) has introduced into the film an erotic energy and sexual fluidity that is hard to contain. According to Rhona Berenstein, queer monsters like Zaleska

> propose a paradigm of sexuality in which eros and danger, sensuality and destruction, human and inhuman, and male and female blur, overlap, and coalesce. In this schema, sexuality and identity remain murky matters, steeped in border crossings and marked by fuzzy boundaries. Thus classic horror may invoke existing definitions of sexuality, but the genre embellishes them with perversions that defy and exceed traditional categories of human desire. (1996: 27)

In other words, films like *Dracula's Daughter* must first conjure up monsters of alternative erotic desire before staking them; but if the cinema has taught us anything at all about vampires, it is that vampires in all their queer glory are impossible to kill completely. The repressed always returns and no matter how dead the vampire looks, he or she will be back in the sequel.

The Era of Lesbian Vampires

In *Dracula's Daughter*, Countess Zaleska is aristocratic and stern-looking. While sexual tension does seem to develop between her and Dr Garth, the locus of conventional feminine beauty is clearly Janet. Garth's rejection of Zaleska − and all that she entails (vampirism/non-standard sexuality/ exotic foreign 'otherness') − is thus validated on several levels as the 'right' choice. But something interesting happens when the spirit of Zaleska reemerges in the late 1960s and early 1970s through an uncanny process of cinematic metempsychosis: she transforms into a sex kitten and her erotic desires take centre-stage. Benshoff traces the 'boomlet' of lesbian vampire movies during this period to the success of Hammer Studios' 'Carmilla'-inspired *The Vampire Lovers* (1970) and describes the formula as follows: 'in a distant and historical European province, the monster arises and feeds, threatens the ingenue [sic] (and/or the normalised heterosexual couple), and is eventually destroyed by patriarchal agents (fathers, priests, generals, boyfriends, etc.)' (1997: 192).

This formula, as almost all of the critics who have considered post-1970 cinematic vampire lesbians have concluded, constructs lesbianism in accordance with the male imaginary and ultimately tend to reinforce negative attitudes toward lesbianism. What Sue-Ellen Case concisely refers to as the 'recreational use of the lesbian' (1991: 2) is addressed by Benshoff, for example, as playing to heterosexual male fantasies (1997: 192). Hanson observes that the scenes of lesbian eroticism in vampire films almost always seem co-opted from straight, male pornography 'in which lesbianism functions as an exotic form of foreplay and exhibitionism, produced primarily for a straight male market' (1999: 184) and this characterisation certainly seems the case for all Hammer Studios' famous lesbian-themed vampire films, including *The Vampire Lovers* (1970), *Lust for a Vampire* (1971) and *Twins of Evil* (1971). Weiss clearly has films such as these in mind when she concludes that lesbian scenes in vampire movies 'invariably cater to male heterosexual fantasy' (1993: 92).

And for the most part, the critics have seen this as a bad thing. Notably, Bonnie Zimmerman argues that the lesbian vampire

> can be used to express a fundamental male fear that female bonding will exclude men and threaten male supremacy. Lesbianism – love between women – must be vampirism; elements of violence compulsion, hypnosis, paralysis, and the supernatural must be present. One woman must be a vampire, draining the life of the other woman, yet holding her in a bond stronger than the grave. (1996: 380)

The message that she reads in the Hammer Studios' films and others is not only that 'lesbianism is sterile and morbid' but also 'if you value your neck, stick with your man' (1996: 380, 382). Jenks arrives at a similar conclusion: 'Lesbianism [in vampire films] is not only violent, 'draining', destructive and power-based [...] but the product of a transferred masculinity or masculine identification' (1996: 123) – that is, lesbian vampires represent gender confusion; they are women who act like men. Addressing the question of how lesbian vampire movies can both titillate and provoke anxiety in straight male viewers, Weiss – who devotes a complete chapter to the topic of vampire lesbians in her book on lesbians in film – asserts that, in keeping with horror movies in general, lesbian vampires produce anxiety which then is relieved at the end with the vampire's destruction. Developing arguments presented by Raymond Bellour and Linda Williams, Weiss concludes that

> the typical lesbian vampire film, belonging within the horror/exploitation genre, is an articulation of men's subconscious fear of and hostility toward women's sexuality. [...] The lesbian vampire film uses lesbianism as titillation that is at once provocative and conquerable, and equates lesbian sexual powers with unnatural powers. (1996: 103–4)

But it strikes me that there is something more complicated – and, frankly, more interesting – going on here. First, as Benshoff points out, the 'lesbians' in almost all lesbian vampires movies are represented as 'hyper-feminine' women rather than stereotyped 'mannish' lesbians (1997: 192) and, as Hanson notes, they are 'more than happy to forgo the state of a woman when an adventurous red-blooded man stumbles on the scene' (1999: 184). These lesbian vampires are in fact not coded as lesbians, but as bisexual and, given the ease with which women are 'seduced' in these films by female vampires, what the films seem to assert is a fundamental female bisexuality. A beautiful woman, these films seem to say, will naturally attract – and be attracted to – both men and women. Furthermore, as I argue is the case with *Dracula's Daughter*, not only do these films conjure up all manner of sexual possibilities that are then impossible to tamp down fully, but the world of patriarchal forces, of 'fathers, priests, generals, boyfriends', often is the world that ends up seeing sterile, bland, lacking and sometimes even downright ugly when compared to the erotic world of the vampire. If anything, it is the 'lesbian' vampires that are especially potent and dangerously attractive, not the patriarchs!

With this in mind, I wish to focus on three 'lesbian vampire' films from 1971 that, rather than displacing the narrative to 'distant and historical' locations, take place within the present and that, through juxtapositions of homosexual and heterosexual object choice, raise interesting questions about the social construction of normalcy and deviance. Each film stages scenes of lesbian sexual intimacy for the purposes of titillating the viewer and, to varying degrees, thus can be construed as exploitation films. Nevertheless, each film also in various ways and to varying extents depicts heterosexuality as bland and restrictive and, in the end, each film allows the sexualised vampire to escape and her erotic energy to continue to circulate.

Vampyros Lesbos

Despite a directorial career running from 1957 to the present and including an astounding 190 films, the work of Spanish director, cinematographer, actor and writer Jesús ('Jess') Franco has received neither commercial success nor much critical discussion. His sexually-charged horror films, however, are cult favourites. *Vampyros Lesbos*, often considered Franco's best film, claims Bram Stoker's story, 'Dracula's Guest', as its inspiration and introduces the theme of the lesbian vampire immediately as it begins with an erotic dance sequence in an upscale Istanbul sex club during which a mysterious, barely-clad brunette (Soledad Miranda) rolls around on the floor of a sparse black stage containing only a large mirror and a candelabra before removing her lingerie and fondling and kissing a naked woman pretending to be a mannequin. The sequence ends with the 'mannequin' prone on the floor and the brunette crouched over her, biting her neck. In the audience are lawyer Linda Westinghouse (Ewa Strömberg) and her boyfriend Omar (Andrés Monales).

Linda is sent from Istanbul to an Anatolian island to handle the inheritance of Countess Nadine Carody (Miranda), heir to the estate of Count Dracula. Nadine (who is the brunette from the sex club, but is not recognised as such by Linda) turns out to be a beautiful woman who has been haunting Linda's dreams and is, of course, a vampire – albeit one that can move about in the daylight. After some frolicking in the sea, nude sunbathing and some possibly drugged wine, Linda, who has passed out and been carried to bed, is awoken by Nadine, who strips, caresses and then bites her. Linda passes out again and when she comes to, finds Nadine floating in her swimming pool, apparently dead; Linda, like a heroine in an Ann Radcliffe novel, passes out for a third time.

When Linda revives this time, she is being treated for amnesia at the clinic of Dr Alwin Seward (Dennis Price). In response to a newspaper advertisement seeking information about Linda, her boyfriend Omar shows up to claim her. Linda remembers him, but nothing about her experience with Countess Carody other than the Countess lying dead in the pool. Nadine, however, is not dead. Instead, the viewer hears her explain to her servant Morpho (José Martínez Blanco), in a scene oddly comparable to a psychoanalytic session and recalling *Dracula's Daughter* that a hundred or two hundred years ago, during a time of political unrest, soldiers broke into her house and attacked her. Count Dracula intervened on her behalf and either saved her from being raped or interrupted the rape (Nadine isn't totally clear on this point) with a dagger in the back of the man who was on top of her. She now hates men and desires to make Linda her companion.

From here, the plot gets even messier. Dr Seward's clinic houses a lunatic named Agra (Heidrun Kussin) – a Renfield-esque character with an intense erotic attraction to Countess Carody – who has been babbling about the 'Queen of the Night' (Nadine) both coming to see her and abandoning her. Nadine does arrive in order to confront Dr Seward about his efforts to separate Linda from her. Dr Seward admits that this was a ruse to provoke Nadine into visiting him because he himself longs to join her in the ranks of the undead. Unfortunately for Dr Seward, things don't work out as planned as Nadine directs Morpho to kill him while she goes to say goodbye to Agra.

Meanwhile, Linda has left the clinic and is on her way back to Nadine's Anatolian beach house when she is attacked and held hostage by Memmet (played by Franco himself), the extremely creepy-looking bellhop at the hotel at which Linda had originally stayed prior to being ferried over to Nadine's beach house. Memmet is a psychopathic sadist who gets off on inflicting pain and has the body of at least one other woman in the wine cellar where he holds Linda captive. Linda manages to outfox and then kill Memmet – who it turns out was Agra's husband before she was seduced by Nadine. Linda completes her trip to Anatolia and finds Nadine there, dying. Linda not only refuses to give her blood to Nadine, but bends over her in such a way as to appear to drink blood from *her*. Then to free herself from Nadine's control, she stabs Nadine in the eye (a method of vampire destruction explained to her by Dr Seward). Nadine's body disappears, Morpho commits suicide, and Omar arrives on the scene and tries to convince Linda it was all a dream, but she knows better. End of movie.

Beyond the messiness of the plot, what stands out about *Vampyros Lesbos* – indeed what is highlighted by the movie's English title – is the ravishing spectacle of lesbian sexuality. Franco's camera is obsessed with the female body and the only thing better in a Franco film than one naked female body is two intertwined. It thus is hard to argue with David Annandale who, in the context of what may be the only sustained academic analysis of *Vampyros Lesbos*, asserts that the film was produced by a man for men. Taking advantage of the relaxing censorship standards of the early 1970s, 'the sex scenes of *Vampyros Lesbos* are the result of a male gaze, and are created for the pleasure of the same' (2002: 262).

And yet at the same time, as Annandale acknowledges, this is overly simplistic. To begin with, the movie starts provocatively with a staging and problematising of the male gaze as Nadine (five years before Anne Rice's 'Théâtre des Vampires' in *Interview With the Vampire*) puts on a show in which she, a vampire, plays a woman, playing a vampire who somehow (in a strange twist on both *Pygmalion* and *Sleeping Beauty*) manages to bring a mannequin, played by a real woman, to life by making love to her, only in order to kill her by sucking her blood as the mixed audience of both men and women claps its approval. This scene is in fact so central to the movie that it is repeated a second time later on.

On the one hand, this is a scene that clearly presents lesbianism as a voyeuristic spectacle structured for the heterosexual male gaze and con-nects 'perverse' sexuality with vampirism – the vampire woman is one who seduces and preys upon feminine beauty. The scene, on the other hand, also arguably undoes these same conclusions by insistently thematising its own artifice – not only does the spectator watch an audience watch a per-formance, but to make things even more complicated, we watch a woman (the actress Soledad Miranda) playing a vampire (Countess Carody) playing a woman playing a vampire (the stage performance). In the process, femi-ninity, lesbianism and vampirism are literally constructed as performative identities; standing naked on stage for the consumption of both the night-club audience and the viewing audience, the actresses – both 'real' and their characters within the film – play their parts: woman as mannequin, woman as woman, woman as vampire. While the narrative within the film works to essentialise lesbianism as deviance, the meta-context of the scene

Vampyros Lesbos: Countess Carody performs

itself complicates this conclusion by foregrounding the social construction of ideas of normalcy and deviance.

Furthermore, in keeping with Benshoff's appraisal of *Dracula's Daughter*, the world of normalcy in *Vampyros Lesbos* is far from appealing for women. Nadine hates men because she was attacked by soldiers before being rescued by Dracula; Memmet gets off on kidnapping, torturing and killing women; Dr Seward dissembles and obscures his true purpose and may be keeping Agra captive to forward his designs; and even Linda's boyfriend, Omar, seems at least as interested in the naked woman on the stage at the club as in the woman by his side. What we are left with is a movie that, although clearly intended to titillate heterosexual male viewers, at the same time foregrounds the destructiveness of that objectifying gaze. The men in the film are as much vampires as is Nadine, and lesbian sex – even vampiric lesbian sex – is presented as far more sensual than heterosexual intimacy.

I do not wish to over-emphasise the progressiveness of *Vampyros Lesbos* as concerns sexuality – this is very obviously a film that caters to male heterosexual fantasy. And while it interestingly redefines female sexuality as intrinsically bisexual, it has little tolerance for women who reject men entirely. Nevertheless, the film fails to provide a satisfactory alternative to lesbianism for women and even as the film reinforces the connection between lesbianism and vampirism, it complicates it by showing that heterosexuality has the potential to be just as vampiric. This is a theme that we will see echoed and elaborated upon in the next two movies discussed, *Requiem for a Vampire* and *Daughters of Darkness*.

Requiem for a Vampire

According to David Kalat, 'Jess Franco's singular obsessions with erotic horror were exceeded by native Frenchman Jean Rollin's career-long fixation on deeply sexual, hideously gory vampire films, suffused with delicate, dreamy poetry' (2002). While *Requiem for a Vampire* lacks gore almost entirely, it clearly exemplifies Rollin's penchant for the surreal and erotic. The film opens with a high-speed chase through the French countryside. Two secondary school-aged girls dressed as clowns and their male driver are being followed by another car and shots are exchanged. The girls' driver is killed, but the girls turn down a country lane and manage to lose their pursuers. To cover their tracks, the seemingly affectless girls set fire to the car – with the dead body of the driver still inside – and, having changed their clothes in a burned-out house, set off by foot across the lonely French countryside. To supply their needs, they turn to theft and subterfuge. They steal a motorcycle and, while blonde-haired Marie (Marie-Pierre Castel) seductively entices a food cart operator away from his truck – the man, it should be noted, requires little prodding to chase her through the woods and seems fully prepared to rape her – brunette Michelle (Mireille Dargent) pilfers from the truck.

When the girls' motorcycle runs out of gas, the movie begins to shift more fully into the surreal mode as the two seek refuge in a cemetery. Surprised by the intrusion of two men, the girls flee and Michelle falls into an open grave and is knocked out. The two men approach the open grave and – in the first of what can be considered many nods to the horror movie tradition – much to Marie's horror, begin to fill it in. Marie watches as, in a sequence calling to mind Carl-Theodor Dreyer's *Vampyr* (1932), Michelle is buried alive. The men quickly finish their work and hurry out of the cemetery while Michelle's hand, in a shot familiar to any horror movie aficionado, emerges zombie-like from beneath the dirt and she claws her way out of the grave with Marie's assistance.

Exiting the cemetery, the two girls are startled by bats in the woods before happening upon an apparently abandoned medieval castle. They explore the labyrinthine interior until they come across a comfortable-looking bed, which – of course – prompts them to strip down for some lesbian love-making and a nap (this is a Rollin film, after all). Awoken by noises, the two stumble into the castle's dungeon and are terrified by a decaying corpse in shackles – shots are fired in a panic at the corpse and then (in a nod toward Jean Cocteau's *Beauty and the Beast* (1946)) at a hand clutching a candlestick emerging from a wall.

Organ music is now heard and the girls enter a chamber in which several cowled figures surround the player. The figures turn out to be skeletons and the player to be an androgynous-looking female vampire (named Erica, played by Dominique Tussaint) with absurd fangs who pursues the girls through the castle and, in a shot clearly an homage to Tod Browning's *Dracula* from 1931, down an imposing castle staircase open on one side. The girls are there cornered by three animalistic male acolytes who – just like the male food cart purveyor encountered earlier – pin the girls down, paw at their clothes and clearly intend to rape them as the head vampire Erica smiles. The girls manage to escape and flee from the castle back to the cemetery where they are again captured and taken to the crypt of the Master Vampire (Paul Bisciglia), an ancient, aristocratic figure – also with absurd fangs – who hypnotises the two girls.

The action then jumps back and forth between two scenes – the interrogation of the two girls by the vampire-in-training Louise (Louise Dhour) in which the girls reveal that they ran off from school, and an extended rape sequence in which the three sadistic and crude male acolytes have their way with shackled female prisoners in the crypt. The women are stripped naked and the vampire Erica feeds not from the neck, but from the breast of one of the victims (an action interestingly also included Hammer Studios' *Twins of Evil* (1971)). The horror of the scene is offset by its sheer absurdity – at one point, a bat is shown on the crotch of one of the female victims.

Marie and Michelle wake up the next morning in the bed they had happened upon initially and then, in a sequence right out of Freud's essay on 'The Uncanny' (1919), they attempt to escape from the castle's grounds, but each path they follow returns them to their starting point. They then form the intention of staking the Master Vampire but are interrupted in the process by Erica. The Master Vampire emerges from his coffin and pronounces the girls' fate – they are to be 'initiated' into vampirism to help replenish their dwindling ranks. Since vampirism is for some reason incommensurate with virginity and the girls are revealed to both be virgins (lesbian sex apparently doesn't count), initiation will consist of deflowering, presumably at the hands of the Master Vampire (although this is left uncertain). In the meantime, the girls will be trained in the ways of the vampire by Louise and since they can still move about during the day, will be sent out to lure victims to the castle.

Michelle turns out to be a very effective hunter. She happens across an older man near the castle and strips naked (except for socks and shoes). The enticed man, as we've come to expect in this film, naturally gives chase and follows her throughout the castle until he encounters Erica who subdues and drinks from him. Michelle drinks as well. Marie's experience is very different; she encounters a handsome young man (Frédéric, played by Philippe Gasté) and entices him to follow her to the castle, but then has reservations both about his fate and hers. She decides that she prefers the idea of losing her virginity willingly to Frédéric than to being forced by the Master Vampire, so the two make love on the ground outside the castle. Marie then returns to the castle and claims she couldn't find anyone to lure inside.

It is now time for the initiation. In an especially absurd and campy scene, Louise plays a grand piano in the graveyard as Michelle goes first into the crypt of the Master Vampire. When she emerges, it is Marie's turn, but she comes scurrying out of the crypt calling for Frédéric when the Master discovers that she is no longer a virgin. While the vampires are searching the castle for Frédéric, Marie returns to the Master's crypt with Frédéric to prove her story about vampires. Frédéric enters and is locked in by the Master Vampire, who then reveals to Marie his secret – he is the last vampire and his ability to create others has waned to the point that only Erica has a chance to complete the change. The others, who have chosen this life because of their 'wild and barbaric' natures, will never become complete vampires.

Unable to open the door to the crypt, Marie returns to the castle where she is confronted and held at gunpoint by Michelle who reminds her how much they love each other and demands to know where Frédéric is. When Marie refuses to say anything, Michelle chains her up in the dungeon, strips her naked, and alternates between whipping her and apologetically kissing her. When Erica threatens one of Marie's eyes with a dagger, Michelle helps her to escape and the two lead everyone back to the Master Vampire's crypt where Frédéric is hiding. As Marie searches for Frédéric, Michelle holds off the vampires-in-training with her gun and they are all killed except for the Master, Erica and Louise. In a surprising twist, Frédéric, having helped fend off the vampires, angrily calls Marie a 'little bitch' for having gotten him involved in this situation and leaves in a huff. The film ends with the Master commanding Louise to seal him and Erica in the tomb and to keep watch. After their deaths, there will be no more vampires.

According to David Pirie, what dominates Rollin's work is 'the conception of vampirism as a luxuriant sexual perversion' (1977: 104). *Requiem for a Vampire*, however, seems to run contrary to this conclusion because 'sexual perversion' is associated most fully not with the vampires, but with the *humans*. To begin with, what the film truly emphasises is the predatory nature of masculine heterosexuality. Except for the girls' driver who is dead in the first five minutes of the film and Frédéric, every man the girls meet wants to rape them. The three male acolytes are exemplary here as the movie's most explicit and outrageous sex scene involves them most directly. They are attracted to vampirism because of their 'wild and barbaric natures' and animalistically leap upon any woman who crosses their path. The food cart purveyor and the man Michelle lures back to the castle also both seem to have little hesitation when it comes to pouncing upon an attractive girl and even Frédéric, who seems an exception to this rule, selfishly turns on Marie and abandons her in the end.

Further, it is arguable that much of the film represents lesbianism as not so much a perversion as an 'immature' form of sexuality – Michelle and Marie, both young schoolgirls, are in love with each other before they arrive at the castle and, as far as the Master Vampire is concerned, lesbian sex doesn't count as real sex – they are both considered virgins. Indeed, right up until the moment when Frédéric abandons Michelle at the crypt (rather than the alter), the film seems as if it is going to be a 'coming of age' story in which both girls graduate from lesbian schoolgirl infatuation into the world of adult heterosexual attraction – Marie 'cheats on' Michelle with Frédéric (which seems to prompt Michelle's torture of her just as much as the desire to discover Frédéric's location) and Michelle has been 'initiated' into heterosexuality, presumably by the Master Vampire. In the end though, both these male figures forsake them. The Master Vampire disappears into his crypt while Frédéric just disappears and the girls are left with each other.

In an odd way, the conclusion of *Requiem for a Vampire* echoes that of *Vampyros Lesbos*: men are either impotent (the Master Vampire) or brutal (all the other men) – or, to put it another way, heterosexual men are the true monsters. Lesbianism – at least as represented by Marie and Michelle – is not only more sensual and gentler than heterosexual intimacy, but less fraught with issues of dominance and control. (It is only once Frédéric enters the picture and the vampires exert their control over Michelle that she turns on Marie.) *Requiem for a Vampire* is thus arguably a lesbian vampire film that decouples 'lesbian' from 'vampire'. The girls are in love with each other to begin with, the vampires try to discipline them into 'mature' and monstrous heterosexuality, but in the end the girls triumph over the forces of darkness and are left with each other. *Requiem for a Vampire* is still, like *Vampyros Lesbos*, a film that delights in representing the naked female form, but again like *Vampyros Lesbos*, it turns the masculine gaze back upon itself by foregrounding its predatory nature.

Daughters of Darkness

My claims above may seem controversial. I am not, however, reading against the grain as much as reading beneath the surface – and it should be pointed out that both *Vampyros Lesbos* and *Requiem for a Vampire* delight in surfaces; each is obviously about skin and the penetration of skin (as are all vampire movies, to varying extents). Both films, however, complicate this emphasis on surfaces by introducing the element of *masquerade*. We have a performance of lesbianism at the start of *Vampyros Lesbos* and two lesbian girls dressed as clowns at the start of *Requiem for a Vampire*. Having foregrounded the staging of lesbianism in each film as performance for the male imaginary, each film then turns the male gaze back upon itself, emphasising its predatory nature. The seat of perversion is thus revealed not to be lesbian intimacy but predatory male heterosexuality.

A third vampire lesbian film from 1971 exemplifies these ideas most fully as it explores the link between sexual desire and vampirism. Directed by Belgian academic and cinema scholar Harry Kümel, *Daughters of Darkness* has been referred to as a 'lesbian vampire art film' (Jenks 1996: 22). The film begins with two newlyweds, Stefan (John Karlen) and Valerie (Danielle Ouimet) Chilton en route from Switzerland to England where Stefan's 'mother' lives. Having just made love, the two play a sort of game in which

Valerie asks Stefan if he loves her and he replies 'No'. Asked the same question, Valerie responds 'Of course I don't'. The tone of their voices and the fact that this is their honeymoon suggests verbal irony; however, subsequent events complicate this interpretation. As a result of a train delay, the couple checks into a fancy hotel in Ostend, Belgium. It is winter and they appear to be the only guests until glamorous Hungarian Countess Elizabeth Bathory (Delphine Seyrig) and her beautiful, exotic secretary Ilona Harczy (Andrea Rau) arrive. The concierge Pierre (Paul Esser) is convinced that this is the same woman he saw forty years earlier when he was working as a bellboy, but clearly this is impossible because she does not appear to have aged a day. The Countess and Ilona quickly take an interest in Stefan and Valerie, and Stefan, who obviously has no interest in taking Valerie to see his 'mother', is happy to prolong their stay in Ostend.

Stefan and Valerie take a day trip to nearby Bruge where they encounter a crowd gathered outside a flat. They learn that a young woman has been murdered – her throat has been cut and the blood drained. And, it turns out, she isn't the first. As the body is carried from the house to a waiting ambulance, an arm falls from beneath the sheet covering the body and a strange look crosses Stefan's face. When Valerie tugs on him to prod him to move along, he hits her as he attempts to free himself. Back at the hotel that evening, the Countess and Stefan have a strange, sexually-charged conversation in which they discuss the various torture techniques the Countess's 'ancestor', the original Countess Bathory, engaged in as she drained young women of their blood to prolong her own youth.

The side of Stefan in which he gets aroused by death and torture is new and disturbing to Valerie – and things only get worse when after Stefan finally calls his 'mother' (who the viewer discovers is a foppish gay man – and, likely, is or has been Stefan's lover), he beats Valerie with a belt and presumably rapes her as well. Valerie packs her bags to leave Stefan, but is intercepted by the Countess at the train station and allows herself to be persuaded to give things another try. In her absence, however, Ilona has seduced Stefan (granted, without much difficulty). After their love-making, Stefan takes a shower and, while trying to pull Ilona under the water with him, ends up killing her as she falls on a straight-edged razor.

The Countess and Valerie return to find Stefan and Ilona's naked bodies lying on the bathroom floor. They take Ilona's body to the shore where Stefan digs a deep hole in the sand while the Countess and Valerie stare

Daughters of Darkness: Valerie and Stefan ... and belt

out at the water from the cliffs above. In one of the film's most striking moments, a long shot shows Valerie standing by the side of the Countess as she raises her arms, her cape spreading out like giant bat wings. Stefan finishes digging the hole, only to find himself pinned under Ilona's body which the Countess has deposited a bit prematurely. As Stefan scrambles to free himself, the sides of the hole begin to collapse threatening to bury Stefan together with Ilona. Luckily for Stefan, Valerie – in a scene similar to the premature burial scene in *Requiem for a Vampire* – still cares for him enough to grasp his hand and help him to extricate himself, even as the Countess appears to be attempting to prevent her from doing so.

Back at the hotel again, Valerie moves into the Countess' room and is shown topless in bed being bitten by the Countess, while Stefan sleeps alone. When asked the next morning by the Countess, playing on the idea of loss of virginity, if it hurt, Valerie responds, 'No, not at all'. Stefan at this point decides to make a last-ditch effort to reclaim his wife from the Countess, asserting to the Countess that 'Valerie will do as I tell her' and, in response to Valerie's barb at him that 'You cannot love, you can only destroy', Stefan grabs her and spits through his teeth at the Countess, 'I am a man and she is mine'. He tries to drag her from the room, Valerie resists, and Stefan again resorts to violence, jumping on top of her and smacking her across the face repeatedly. Elizabeth joins Valerie in attempting to fend off Stefan and the two of them cover his face with a large glass bowl that breaks in the struggle and conveniently cuts both his wrists. What follows is the most graphic scene of vampirism in the movie as both the Countess and Valerie pounce on Stefan and drink from the wounds.

Now time is of the essence because they must dispose of the body before dawn. Stefan's shrouded body (after being thrown unceremoniously from the balcony to the ground below with a thud) is dumped in a marsh but, as Valerie and the Countess rush back to the hotel, the breaking dawn's light strikes the speeding car and Valerie loses control and crashes. The Countess is thrown from the car and impaled on a tree branch. This would seem to be the end of things but, after an intertitle reading 'a few months later', we see Valerie walking arm and arm with a young couple, telling them how they will be the best of friends. The voice we hear, however, is not Valerie's but the Countess's.

Daughters of Darkness is a film, like *Vampyros Lesbos*, in which the central female protagonist is caught in a love triangle between two vampires – in this case, the 'actual' vampire, Countess Bathory, and the figurative vampire, her husband Stefan. (That Stefan should be considered a vampire is the gist of several apparent allusions to Bram Stoker's novel. For example, when Valerie tells him 'You cannot love, you can only destroy', the spectator conversant with Stoker may recall the comment from Dracula's brides that 'You yourself never loved; you never love!' (1997: 43). Further, Stefan's assertion that he is a man and Valerie is his possession recalls Dracula's taunt that England's women are his already.) The strange *tête-à-tête* in which the Countess and Stefan get turned on discussing torture techniques establishes that both are sadists, and both seek to possess and control Valerie. Further, both are associated with 'perverse' sexuality – the Countess is attracted to beautiful young women while Stefan, who clearly has an unorthodox relationship with 'mother' (one can't say for sure whether they have been lovers, but this does seem to be implied – Zimmerman refers to Stefan as the 'kept man of an elderly transvestite' (1996: 385)), seems unable to perform in the bedroom without contemplating torture and/or beating his wife first.

Both the Countess and Stefan also are good examples of what I have been calling the hyperbolic gender of the vampire. This is most apparent with the Countess who is for all intents and purposes a woman in *drag* – a woman performing a caricature of femininity. Almost all commentators on *Daughters of Darkness* note Delphine Seyrig's delightfully campy performance which, as Zimmerman observes, 'dissipates some of the Gothic atmosphere' (1996: 386). In the midst of the empty hotel, the Countess appears swathed in glamorous gowns, all fur and feathers. In the sequence leading up to Stefan's death, she emerges dramatically into Stefan and Valerie's suite from behind the balcony doors (how did she get there?) armoured in a dazzling, slinky metallic dress. She is a spectacle. Here, she is, as Jenks appreciates, 'femininity in masquerade' as she 'caresses her hair, her body, and her postures are more swan-like than ever, back arched, arms flung out' (1996: 32). The camp value is then accentuated still further as the Countess melodramatically foregrounds her own performance describing herself as 'an outmoded character, nothing more. You know, the beautiful stranger, slightly sad, slightly mysterious, that haunts one place after another.' This aging drag queen's performance would be comically pathetic were it not for the knowledge of the power she possesses and her dramatic contrast with the dishevelled scowling presence of Stefan, garbed only in a rust-coloured bath robe.

Although both the Countess and Stefan are portrayed as vampires, Stefan is the film's true monster. Perhaps compensating as Zimmerman and Jenks both suggest for his homosexual tendencies, he too becomes a hyperbolic representation of gender – in this instance of masculine aggression, abusing his 'male "privilege" of establishing control over his woman' (Zimmerman 1996: 385), revealing the violence inherent in marriage (Jenks 1996: 29), and recasting the 'heterosexual norm' as 'frighteningly abnormal and nightmarish' (Weiss 1993: 101). Although both the Countess and Stefan share an attraction to pain and death and both contend for Valerie, Stefan is represented as coarse, brutal and unsympathetic, while the Countess is 'portrayed as being a sophisticated, intelligent, motherly, and fascinating woman' (Zimmerman 1996: 386). Her's ultimately is the more appealing performance and while the film at times suggests that the Countess exercises a sort of hypnotic control over Valerie, her preference for the Countess isn't hard to comprehend. According to Zimmerman, the film shows 'lesbianism as attractive and heterosexuality as abnormal and ineffectual' (ibid.). Crucial to this feminist interpretation is the brief conclusion to the film in which Valerie reappears speaking with the Countess's voice. It appears that the spirit of the Countess has moved on to a new, younger body: 'the stiff-faced beauty queen, whom we have seen as innocent bride, passive masochist, and fascinated victim, is now the powerful, immortal lesbian vampire' (ibid.).

Vampyros Lesbos, Requiem for a Vampire and *Daughters of Darkness* stage scenes of lesbian attraction and intimacy for the viewer and all three have been characterised as lesbian vampire movies. In each case, the association of lesbianism with vampirism participates in the construction of the vampire as a sexual monster – a perverse sexual monster that enacts a tabooed and titillating sexual identity. And, to varying extents, critics are right to suggest that this association reinforces the homophobic demonisation of homosexuals. At the same time though, as I hope to have shown, even in a film such as *Vampyros Lesbos* that clearly seems to belong in the exploitation category, there is a countervailing force at work that not only renders lesbianism attractive through its juxtaposition with unflattering representations of heterosexuality, but that reveals gender itself – including the expectation of 'correct' sexual object choice – to be both performative and unstable.

Interview With the Vampire

I will conclude this chapter by briefly discussing the 1994 adaptation of Anne Rice's bestselling novel from 1976, *Interview With the Vampire*, which, despite the fact that it isn't in my opinion an especially good vampire movie, must be numbered among the most provocative not just because of the association it develops between vampirism and male homosexuality but because of the positive valence it gives to this association. The simple fact of the matter is that, while there is a whole sub-tradition of lesbian vampire movies, outside of gay pornography there are remarkably few gay vampire movies. Richard Dyer interestingly suggests that this is because the Gothic tradition constructs a 'natural' space for lesbianism, while no such space exists for male homosexuality: 'it may be that lesbian vampires/lesbian Gothic is a continuation of aspects of female culture, whereas gay vampires/gay Gothic is a deviation from male culture' (1988: 50). Although Dyer does not develop this assertion extensively, his point is that lesbians share with women in general a sense of disenfranchisement in patriarchal culture and, further, lesbian intimacy is perceived to be the extension of the emotional and physical intimacy permitted to women; in contrast, straight (white) men do not share marginalised status with gay men, nor do cultural codes allow straight men to express affection through physical contact or displays of emotionality. Thus, 'lesbian Gothic extends forms and feelings well developed within women's writing as a whole; whereas gay Gothic is precisely not like men's writing' (ibid.).

When considering vampire cinema, however – overwhelmingly the product of male writers, directors and producers – it seems clear that the scenes of lesbian intimacy, as discussed above, are specifically included to titillate male spectators. Scenes featuring 'hyper-feminine' women engaging in various erotic activities play to the male pornographic desire to intervene and, as Zimmerman suggests, to demonstrate sexual prowess and masculine superiority while being serviced by compliant women (1996: 385). While such scenes, as I have argued, may indeed introduce a queer energy that continues to circulate even after the vampire is staked (with all the phallic implications of staking), in most cases heterosexual anxiety elicited by the prospect of sexual relations excluding men is dispelled: 'By showing the lesbian as a vampire-rapist who violates and destroys her victim, men alleviate their fears that lesbian love could create an alternate model, that two women without coercion or morbidity might prefer one another to a man' (Zimmerman 1996: 382).

In contrast to the *joie de vivre* that the vampire cinema has taken in portraying scenes of lesbian homoeroticism, there has been little tolerance – in keeping with cinematic history in general – for *male* homoeroticism. In an important article on Bram Stoker's *Dracula*, Christopher Craft (1984) makes a persuasive case that the true anxiety underlying the novel is the lurking fear that Dracula – who despite his monstrosity, maintains a decorous heterosexuality – might bite and penetrate *a man*. The novel of course does some interesting things with gender – Jonathan Harker takes the place of the conventional Gothic heroine trapped in the spooky castle and constantly in danger of being raped, Mina Harker in contrast takes on a very masculine role in the pursuit of Dracula – but Dracula (as the 1979 'sexy Dracula' adaptation with Frank Langella makes clear) is ultimately a ladies' man defined by his potency and (heterosexual) animal magnetism.

It does need to be acknowledged that, in the vampire cinema, there are plenty of representations of male vampires biting men, so given the sexual overtones of the vampiric bite, homoeroticism would seem to be implicit. This anxiety, however, is addressed by either having the attacks take place off-screen or coding them as brutal rather than sensual. In addition, attacks on male victims are not repeated and the male victim is never shown to desire or enjoy the attack. Consider Hammer Studios' *Horror of Dracula* (1958) as a case in point. Christopher Lee's vampirisation of Jonathan Harker (John Van Eyssen) (who in this adaptation of Stoker's novel has travelled to Castle Dracula specifically to destroy the vampire) is never shown. When Dracula makes his moves on Lucy (Carol Marsh), however, she seems eager for his visit and he hovers hungrily over her before moving in for a nibble. Thus, we arrive at the following matrix governing the history of vampire cinema: female vampire biting female victim = very sexy; female vampire biting male victim = very sexy; male vampire biting female victim = quite sexy; male vampire biting male victim = NOT sexy. What we see here are the limits of the male cinematic imagination and the true taboo underlying the vampire genre – male homosexuality.

It is because the vampire genre has tried so hard to exclude the possibility of male/male same-sex attraction that *Interview With the Vampire* is so fascinating – not only does the film depict the homoeroticism that the history of vampire cinema has tried to disguise, but it revels in it by casting as its central characters actors generally recognised for their good looks: Brad Pitt, Tom Cruise, Antonio Bandaras, Christian Slater and Stephen Rea. And perhaps even more astonishingly, their gayness is played 'straight' – that is, unlike the abysmal *To Wong Foo Thanks for Everything, Julie Newmar* which came out one year later in 1995 with Hollywood sex symbols Wesley Snipes and Patrick Swayze dressed in drag as a big joke, *Interview With the Vampire* arguably excludes irony in its representations of the interactions between its big-name sexy male actors. As in Rice's novel, the movie tells Louis' coming-out story – his attempt to grapple with, understand and come to terms with his 'perverse' vampiric nature.

Interview With the Vampire, I am tempted to say, thus pulls the sheet away from the vampire cinema's Dorian Gray portrait, highlighting the inherent queerness of the vampire genre by suggesting (as does the character Stefan in *Daughters of Darkness*) that the masculine vampire's misogynistic attack on women is a reflection of anxiety generated his own gender confusion. And, as Eve Sedgwick has developed in *Between Men* (1985) in relation to canonical literary texts from Shakespeare to Tennyson, the 'classic' vampire plot really boils down to a contest between men for control of women in which the women themselves are really interchangeable ciphers. *Interview With the Vampire* does away with the middleman, or rather middlewoman, and allows the vampire to pursue his true desire – another man. The underlying anxiety of Stoker's novel thus finally finds expression just about one hundred years later. The super-sexy male vampire is outed as gay.

Conclusion

The point of this chapter has been that, whether man or woman, gay, straight or bisexual, the cinematic vampire is always an embodiment of excessive, tabooed sexuality. As such, the vampire is always 'queer' inasmuch as it makes clear (or demythologises) the cultural codes that define normative sexuality and shows them not to be natural at all, but cultural constructions. Film's first vampires were vamps, women who put their sexuality to work to fulfil their own desires by controlling men. Stephen Prince asserts that the famous version of *Dracula* from 1931 starring Bela Lugosi shifted the connotation of vampire away from vamp and back to undead supernatural (male) creature (2004: 58), but it also highlighted both the predatory heterosexuality of the vampire (David J. Hogan refers to Lugosi's Dracula as a 'sexual criminal' (1986: 138)) and his queer potential – in this contest for control of women, the women themselves are virtually interchangeable non-entities. The film's real energy is the contest between Dracula and the men who pursue him, which includes the memorable scene of Dracula's failed 'seduction' of Van Helsing (Edward Van Sloan)!

The queer valence of the vampire – the vampire as problematic metaphor for tabooed sexuality – is developed even more fully by the lesbian vampire tradition. Particularly in the films of the late 1960s and 1970s, hyper-feminine and hyper-sexualised lesbian vampires compete with men for control of their women. While products of heterosexual male fantasy who generally get punished for their deviance, these lesbian vampires – powerful and seductive – highlight the policing force of patriarchal culture and raise interesting questions about cinematic enjoyment. Feminist film critics such as Laura Mulvey and Linda Williams have offered very powerful analyses of the ways in which traditional Hollywood cinema objectifies women and demonises female sexuality – and films in which vampire lesbians seduce other women and then get staked would seem to be cases in point. However, Ellis Hanson, while not disputing these claims, nonetheless asserts that lesbian vampire films hold 'enormous potential for queer narrative pleasure' (1999: 219) and, extending Hanson's meditations, we can ask questions including: Is it necessarily 'illegitimate' or misogynistic for a male heterosexual spectator to become aroused watching an intimate scene involving two women? Can queer viewers still derive enjoyment from such a scene, even if it obviously plays to straight male desire? What if the spectator is a 'straight' woman or 'gay' man? And what of a film like *Interview With the Vampire* in which the vampires are obviously queer? Or a film like *Twilight* that shows us that the only way to be a complete man is to be a monster?

This is part of the complexity of the vampire film – few of them are either wholly repressive or entirely subversive. Instead, they mostly occupy an uncanny sexual hinterland, a liminal space in which sexuality is represented as a fraught and complicated matter. What the vampire film offers (in keeping with the cinema in general) is a psychic screen for the projection and staging of desire; and what vampire films show us is that sexual desire is amorphous and fluid until channelled by cultural expectations in certain prescribed directions. Nevertheless, that desire always possesses the potential to overflow the dams blocking its path and to spread out in other directions. The vampire finally both attracts and repulses due to its excessive, tabooed sexuality. Evoking the thrill of a forbidden sexuality, always more appealing than the men and women who hunt it, uncannily more alive than we are, the vampire gives shape to repressed and/or tabooed sexual desire and parades it across the screen. And if we learn anything from the vampire cinema it is that once the vampire's crypt has been opened, it is impossible to close completely.

2   VAMPIRE TECHNOLOGY

At the end of April 2009, panic erupted around the globe over the possible epidemic spread of Swine Flu. Originating in Mexico, which more or less shut down during the height of the panic, cases were reported in places as far-flung as New Zealand, Spain and Japan. In response, the World Health Organization raised its pandemic alert scale to 5 out of 6 (it subsequently went to phase 6), meaning human-to-human spread of the virus has been reported in at least two countries and that a pandemic is likely, leading various government and multi-national organisations to mobilise in order to treat and check the spread of an illness many people – including myself – had never heard of before. At least I thought I had never heard of it before. As it turns out, I was wrong.

Coincidentally, in the midst of the Swine Flu panic, I was re-watching David Cronenberg's innovative 1977 revisioning of the vampire story, *Rabid*. I had already been impressed with this film's uncanny prescience as it's a film that seems to predict with astonishing accuracy both the AIDS crisis (which wasn't even a blip on the radar in 1977) and contemporary debates over stem cell research. To summarise the film briefly (I will deal with it in more depth later), as a result of a bad motorcycle accident, the semi-unwitting antagonist Rose, played by porn star Marilyn Chambers, receives an internal graft of 'morphogenetically neutral' skin which the doctor, Dan Keloid (Howard Ryshpan), compares to embryonic tissue – stem cells. A mutation occurs causing Rose to develop a new organ under her arm – a sphincter-like orifice with a retractable stinger or pricker of sorts (call it Rose's thorn) that sucks blood. After Rose feeds off some hapless victim, the victim becomes infected, rapidly sickens, foams at the mouth, and attacks other people before dying – those attacked then sicken and foam and attack other people and die and so on. The authorities, who initially conceive of the epidemic illness as a rabies variant, determine that the illness is spread through the saliva of infected persons. Martial law is declared in Montreal, the epicentre of the illness, and in a clear parallel with George A. Romero's *Night of the Living Dead* (1968) – a film to which *Rabid* is heavily indebted – the only way to deal with the aggressive zombie-like virus victims is to shoot them.

Looking back, the film is startlingly prophetic. Dr Keloid performs experimental surgery using the equivalent of stem cells, creating a vampire. The result of his 'unnatural' intervention, a monstrous male/female hybrid played by a porn star with a blood-sucking vagina-penis-anus under its arm, is patient zero for a new epidemic disease spread through the sexualised (at least in Rose's case) exchange of saliva – those she seduces as she walks the streets in her fur coat and pricks with her unnatural pricker become infected and spread that infection to others by biting them. All of this seems to prefigure the AIDS crisis that exploded only a few years later. And the kicker: in the early stages of the spread of the epidemic, a Canadian health official interviewed on television, attempting to stress the gravity of the situation, states 'this is no outbreak of Swine Flu'. It turns out I had heard of Swine Flu before 2009 – roughly 15 years earlier while watching on VHS a vampire movie from 1977 that ups the ante, so to speak, concerning vampirism as a sexually transmitted disease by turning it into a potentially global pandemic.

David Pirie, in a book coincidentally published in the same year that *Rabid* was released, opined that the vampire movie had run its course and, like *Nosferatu*'s Count Orlok exposed to sunlight, was about to disappear in a little puff of smoke. But despite all the vampire movies Pirie had watched, he somehow missed the essential vampire message: you just can't keep a good vampire down for long. However insightful Pirie's analysis of vampire cinema (and the book really is quite good), Cronenberg's *Rabid*, (along with another vampire movie released in 1977, Romero's *Martin*, to be discussed in the next chapter), effectively undermines any faith in his prognosticative abilities, making clear that that the vampire, even though conventionally associated with the past, is always a creature of the present looking toward the future. The vampire cinema may wax and wane, but one of the main rules concerning the undead is that they always return – usually just when you've let your guard down.

The reason for the vampire's inevitable resurrection is that vampire movies insistently engage with a certain set of recurring themes and issues that just never go out of style. In the last chapter, I dealt with sex and the argument was that vampires are indelibly marked in the contemporary imagination as the sexiest of monsters to such an extent that it seems impossible to think about the cinematic vampire today without on some level also considering sexual mores and taboos; when we think celluloid vampires, we think sex. The ideas have become so inextricably intertwined that it seems natural and obvious to relate one to the other. The movies, together with popular literature, have created a sex(y) monster.

The argument of this chapter is perhaps a bit less immediately obvious. *Rabid* is clearly about sex; the vampire in this movie, however, is not a supernatural creature, but the product of scientific experimentation. What I will be arguing here is that, just as much as with sex, the cinematic vampire is also intimately intertwined in the popular imagination with ideas about science and technology. The silver-screen vampire, itself a product of cinema technology, is inevitably defined in relation to various technologies of representation, definition, detection and destruction. As such, the cinematic vampire is a creature constructed by, in relation to, and against contemporary conceptualisations of technology. The argument here is thus that when we think of movie vampires, we are also on some level thinking about the conflicted human relationship to tools, science and the cinema itself. I will pursue this topic of what I will call the technologised vampire in two directions: I will start by considering vampire films that place science and technology centre-stage thereby making obvious what is more or less the case for every vampire film. This will include films such as *The Last Man on Earth* (1964), its remake *I Am Legend* and *Rabid*, films that redefine vampirism as a contagious disease that can be treated and cured, as well as films including *Blade* and *Van Helsing* that showcase scientific approaches to developing vampire prophylactics and eradicants. These are vampire movies that focus much of their attention on the perils and promises of science and clearly relate one to the other.

Then this chapter will move in a metatextual direction as it considers the cinema itself as a form of 'vampire technology'. Here I will argue not only that the cinematic vampire is first and foremost a celluloid entity, a product of special effects, creative editing and a variety of cinematic tricks of the trade, but that, thinking in the reverse direction, the cinema also must be conceived of as a vampiric creation – that is, the vampire, present at the birth of cinema, has shaped our thinking about the cinema. The same cinematic apparatus that raises the dead drains life from the living and all vampire cinematic texts to varying extents circle back upon themselves, underlining the cinema itself as a vampiric medium. With this in mind, I will start with the fascinating scene from Francis Ford Coppola's *Bram Stoker's Dracula* in which the Count (Gary Oldman) and Mina Harker (Winona Ryder) literally go to the movies, before focusing on F. W. Murnau's *Nosferatu* and Carl-Theodor Dreyer's *Vampyr*, which are both pioneering films that foreground the vampiric possibilities of film. Then I will loop back around in time to another film in which the vampire goes to the movies – the movie that most explicitly equates the vampire with cinematic technology, E. Elias Merhinge's delightful *Shadow of the Vampire* (2000). Finally, the chapter will round things out with some consideration of what certainly is one of the oddest films to be considered in this study – and one that clearly makes the connection between technology and vampirism – Guillermo del Toro's *Cronos*. What I hope to show by the end is that cinematic vampires are inevitably 'technological' – when we 'think' the vampire cinema, we are always on some level thinking about our relationships with science and technology.

Detection, Identification, Destruction

In Rob Latham's excellent study, *Consuming Youth: Vampires, Cyborgs, & the Culture of Consumption* (2002), drawing his inspiration from Karl Marx, Latham argues that vampires and cyborgs are historically connected and, indeed, that they function as two sides of the same coin with – in my extremely crude rendering of his sophisticated argument – vampires figuring as avid capitalists, and cyborgs (individuals whose physiological functioning is aided by or dependent upon mechanical or electronic devices) standing in for the exploited masses. My assertion here, which draws some of its inspiration from Latham, is that the vampire and cyborg are not just complementary images, but that vampires are themselves inherently cybernetic creations, flesh-machine syntheses defined and produced by various technologies. The cinematic vampire is always already a type of cyborg.

We can begin to develop this thesis by noting that, from its folkloric roots to its present-day cinematic incarnations, the vampire has all along been associated with various technologies of detection, identification and destruction. Re-emphasising the role of the slayer in vampire folklore, Bruce A. McClelland observes in *Slayers and Their Vampires: A Cultural History of Killing the Dead* that Eastern European folkloric accounts focus not on the destruction of the vampire – the slayer in fact seldom encounters any real resistance (see 2006: 113) – but rather on the determination of the problem and the identification of the vampire and his location. Similarly, every vampire movie on some level invariably asks the question of the nature of the vampire and its relation to the world that we know. The explicit questions are 'what is this creature?' and 'what are its weaknesses?' The implicit question is 'how does the existence of this creature challenge or reinforce accepted narratives of how the world works?' The trajectory of most vampire films aims toward answering these questions, often entertaining and discarding a variety of possibilities along the way. One first needs to determine that what one is dealing with is a vampire, then one must figure out who (and what) the vampire is, and lastly one must discover how to treat the vampire's victims and destroy the vampire. This involves a process of ratiocination – of deliberate reasoning – but it also invariably involves *tools* ranging from seemingly archaic ones such as wooden stakes, hawthorn branches, holy water and crosses to modernised variants including engineered anti-vampire viruses, laser-like 'UV arcs', garlic-infused vampire repellent spray and light grenades. The vampire is thus an entity defined by its relation to and association with various specific technologies, primitive as they may be, of creation and destruction.

In the process of defining and strategising how to combat the vampire, the vampire frequently gets constructed as an agent of disease and vampirism defined as a type of virus or infection. As in my preliminary discussion of *Rabid* above – or as we shall see with *The Last Man on Earth* and *I Am Legend* – the protagonists racing against time to stop the spread of the vampire affliction are more or less explicitly cast as scientists racing to stop the spread of a potential pandemic (or, in the case of *Blade: Trinity*, to develop their own anti-vampire virus). The figuring of the vampire as a plague, virus, sickness or pandemic thus stages a confrontation with conceptions of the nature and limits of science and thematises the human relationship with technology. When we ask what the vampire is, we are asking an ontological question that may or may not complicate our understanding of how the world works; when we ask how to track and destroy the vampire, we are asking epistemological questions that inevitably intersect with the human relationship with technology.

The Infectious Vampire

The Last Man on Earth

I suggested in the Introduction to this book that the vampire family tree has three branches (natural, unnatural, supernatural) that figure the ways in which the vampire film spreads out and colonises – or vampirises – other genres; nevertheless, regardless of the vampire's ontological status, it tends to be engaged through the same process: detection, definition and then determination of course of action. Vampires of all stripes – in keeping with monsters in movies more generally – are a problem that need to be solved. In order to address this problem, one marshals knowledge from a variety of sources (folklore, experts, literature, movies, experimentation) and develops appropriate tools. This inherent relationship of the vampire to technologies of detection, determination and destruction, however, has been increasingly emphasised in what we may call the 'infection vampire' film and the 'action vampire' film. In the infection vampire film, the vampire is recast as a naturally occurring or scientifically created pandemic that must be battled through scientific means. Action vampire movies emphasise the increasingly sophisticated tools used to track and destroy vampires.

The pioneering infection vampire film is *The Last Man on Earth* from 1964, starring Vincent Price. This cinematic adaptation of Richard Matheson's 1954 vampire novel, *I Am Legend*, features a post-apocalyptic world in which a virus has turned everyone into a vampire – everyone that is except for Dr Robert Morgan (Price) who spends his days destroying vampires and attempting to understand the plague that has ravaged the planet. Morgan offers scientific explanations for vampire behaviour and concludes that his own resistance to the virus stems from having been bitten by an infected vampire bat while stationed in Panama, in essence inoculating him. Vampirism is thus redefined as an infection of the blood; there is nothing supernatural about it.

While out hunting vampires one day, Morgan discovers Ruth (Franca Bettoia) – since the whole world has been transformed into vampires unable to tolerate sunlight, this is unexpected. Ruth, it turns out, is part of a population of living people who are infected with the vampirism virus, but who have developed a course of treatment that mitigates the symptoms and who are planning to rebuild society. They fear Morgan who somehow has remained unaffected by the virus and moves about during the day while they are sleeping, unwittingly killing their people. Ruth has been sent to spy on Morgan and, while she is unconscious, Morgan transfuses his blood into her, which cures her; this leads Morgan to hope that the rest of the living vampires can be cured as well. Alas, things end badly for Morgan. Ruth's people attack and Morgan, who flees from his home, is cornered in a church where he, 'the last true man on earth', is impaled on the altar by a spear and he famously shouts before he dies, 'Freaks! You're all freaks!'

What distinguishes the 1964 version with Vincent Price from both the 1971 adaptation with Charlton Heston (*The Omega Man*) and the more recent 2007 version, *I Am Legend*, starring Will Smith is the retention (albeit in somewhat watered-down form) of Matheson's astonishing trick ending in which it is revealed that the book's protagonist, Robert Neville (renamed Morgan in *The Last Man on Earth*) is the text's true monster, destroying vampires in their sleep. What Matheson's ending vividly illustrates is that normalcy is entirely a social construction. If everyone drinks blood and sleeps during the day, drinking blood and sleeping during the day become the norm. It is not the vampires who are freaks in *The Last Man on Earth*, but Morgan, the only non-vampire left.

For our purposes here, however, what is also especially significant about *The Last Man on Earth* is that, in keeping with Matheson's Cold War-era novel that implies that the vampire plague resulted from environmental destruction stemming from modern technologies of warfare including nuclear and biological weapons, it treats vampirism scientifically as a type of disease that can be cured medically. In this movie version, as in both *The Omega Man* and *I Am Legend*, the protagonist is a medical researcher who engages in a process of scientific exploration seeking to understand the cause and course of treatment for the disease. Although vampirism going back to Bram Stoker's novel was pathologised as a disease of the blood, *The Last Man on Earth* redefines the etiology of the illness from supernatural to natural – vampirism is caused by a virus resulting from human manipulation of nature; it is purely scientific. In addition, vampirism itself ultimately is redefined twice – from supernatural to unnatural and ultimately to natural.

All human beings in this post-apocalyptic world have become bloodsuckers so vampirism is the new norm.

What *The Last Man on Earth*, *The Omega Man* and *I Am Legend* foreground is the vexed human relationship with technology – both its peril and its promise. In these films, modern technology creates vampires and modern technology is called upon to combat vampires. The vampire in these films is thus interestingly reconceived as a sort of cyborg – although not literally part flesh and part machine, these vampires are nonetheless every bit as technologised as Frankenstein's monster or the Terminator. They are products of the lab, offspring of science's tampering with nature. The altered blood that one sees when one looks through the microscope – a now clichéd vampire film shot recurring from *Rabid* to *Blade* – is the visual evidence of scientific manipulation. The vampire, in short, is the offspring of modern technology.

Rabid

David Cronenberg's *Rabid*, perhaps the bleakest version of the vampire infection movie, can be considered a sort of prequel to *The Last Man on Earth* in that it documents the start of a vampire plague rather than its aftermath. In this film, the vampire plague is not a result of nuclear or germ warfare, but of ethically questionable medical experimentation gone awry. As summarised at the start of this chapter, Rose (Marilyn Chambers) is involved in a motorcycle crash with her boyfriend and sustains major injuries. She is taken in a coma to a nearby medical clinic where Dr Dan Keloid performs experimental surgery on her, grafting 'morphogenetically neutral' patches of her own skin on to (and into) the injured areas of her chest and abdomen. The new skin – essentially stem cells – will have the ability to become whatever type of tissue to which it is grafted, but also holds the risk of becoming cancerous. Cancer, the viewer discovers, would have been preferable considering what happens next.

Rose emerges from her coma with a new orifice located where skin was grafted near her armpit. The sphincter-like orifice features a retractable stinger that emerges to pierce her victims and suck their blood. A few hours after being bitten, Rose's victims froth at the mouth and then go berserk, attacking and biting others – who then undergo the same changes and the virus spreads. The local authorities, perplexed and overwhelmed, conclude that they are facing an outbreak of rabies. Meanwhile, things go from bad to worse at the Keloid Clinic when Rose feeds sequentially upon several patients there for plastic surgery and then upon Dr Keloid himself – who in the film's goriest scene goes insane while performing surgery. During the mayhem Rose escapes and heads to Montreal to stay with her friend Mindy (Susan Roman) where she continues to feed unchecked, slipping outside periodically in her luxurious fur coat for some 'fresh air' and walking the streets in search of victims. Montreal imposes a state of martial law and vaccinates citizens against rabies, but the shots do not work. Rose's boyfriend Hart (Frank Moore) discovers her feeding on Mindy and accuses her of being the source of the epidemic, calling her 'Typhoid Mary'. Rose, who is aware of her predatory activity but seemingly not of its results, tests this theory by feeding on a man with whom she is locked in a room to see if he becomes sick. The next day, her body is found lying next to some trashcans and is unceremoniously dumped in the back of a garbage truck as the end credits role.

Rabid, as noted above, is clearly indebted both in terms of style and themes to George A. Romero's Night of the Living Dead. In that film, radiation from a space probe that explodes in earth's atmosphere is credited with animating the recently deceased, who then attack the living and engage in acts of cannibalism. Several refuges from the mayhem hole up in an empty farmhouse and must fend off the cannibalistic zombies while also contending with each other. In the end, the sole survivor of the harrowing night, Ben (Duane Jones), the film's heroic black protagonist, is mistaken for a zombie and shot dead by a roving band of zombie killers – a textbook example of tragic irony. Rabid shares with Night of the Living Dead a scientifically-created vampire pandemic, 'infected' monsters quickly killed by gunfire, and a brutal anticlimax in which in the film's central figure is abruptly and unceremoniously dispatched (and, one could argue, Night of the Living Dead's sequel, Dawn of the Dead (1978), in turn borrows a shopping mall scene from Rabid). However, whereas Night of the Living Dead has been convincingly interpreted as condensing anxieties about the American war in Vietnam, 1960s race relations and the generation gap, Rabid arguably derives its motor force from unapologetic misogyny and anxieties about 'unnatural' science escaping human control.

As discussed in Chapter One, fear of female sexuality has been an organising theme of the vampire cinema since its inceptions and can be traced back all the way to A Fool There Was from 1915. Rabid, however – in keeping with the 'body horror' of Cronenberg (see Hurley 1995: 203) – develops this theme in an especially graphic way. Rose's unnatural new organ combines vagina with penis. It is a sphincter-like hole concealing a monstrous appendage. When Rose seduces her victims with what Ira Livingston describes as her 'hypersexualised embraces' (1993), her prick emerges to penetrate and suck their blood. It seems wholly in keeping with the film's panic regarding women's active sexuality that the owner of the killer orifice should be a porn star whose monstrous organ promiscuously sucks the life out of others and spreads disease. Indeed, at one point Rose actually goes in search of victims at an adult movie house. Rose meanwhile is curiously affectless in the process as her orifice takes over and, despite the fact that her plastic surgery was non-elective (she was in a coma at the time it was performed), no sympathy is offered for her. The film sucks her dry in the same way that she sucks others dry and ends with her body being literally tossed into a garbage truck. Just another one for the fire, as the hick sheriff in *Night of the Living Dead* might say.

Beyond this all-too-familiar fear of unchecked female sexuality, however, the film's bleakness inheres in its caustic appraisal of modern science. Dr Keloid performs elective plastic surgery at his fancy clinic and his patients are shown to be both vain and insecure, altering themselves again and again in what may be one of the cinema's earliest depictions of what has come to be called 'body dysmorphic disorder', dissatisfaction with one's body leading to plastic surgery addiction. When Rose is brought in after her accident, an experimental procedure is performed on her without her knowledge or consent and, as a result, she is transformed into a monster – a sort of hermaphroditic bisexual she-male who derives her life-force by literally draining the life-force of others. Her engineered monstrosity – Hurley calls Rose a 'cyborgic entity' (1995: 214) – then precipitates a sexualised pandemic as she becomes 'patient zero', the film's Typhoid Mary, infecting others with a virus that spreads through biting and contaminated saliva. At the end of the film, Rose is dead and it seems that the authorities are gaining the upper hand on the pandemic, although nothing can be done for the victims except to shoot them. The cause of the outbreak, however, has not been discovered or isolated and it presumably will only be a matter of time until the next outbreak of some monstrous scientifically engineered pandemic.

I Am Legend
The thirty-year jump from *Rabid* to *I Am Legend* turns out to be a short one. Indeed, *I Am Legend* effectively combines *The Last Man on Earth* with *Rabid* in presenting human medical experimentation as unleashing a vampire plague that ravages the planet. Despite this discouraging premise, *I Am Legend* – in clear conformity with big-budget Hollywood summer block-buster releases – refuses to be as cynical as either *The Last Man on Earth* or *Rabid*. The plague that afflicts humanity in *I Am Legend* is neither the result of nuclear war nor unsanctioned surgery; rather, it is the unintended conse-quence of a medical treatment – a mutation of a genetically reengineered measles virus designed to wipe out cancer. It is benevolence gone awry, not the lamentable consequence of human hostility or ethically question-able surgery. And in *I Am Legend*, despite its riffing on Matheson, Robert Neville (Will Smith) is not the last man on earth; in the ending included with the general release of the film (which is indebted much more to *The Omega Man* than to either Matheson or *The Last Man on Earth*), enclaves of humans remain unaffected and, through Neville's efforts, are able to develop a vaccine to protect themselves. In addition, in what I think is perhaps the most significant deviation from Matheson's novel – and the infection vampire subgenre in general – the diseased human beings in *I Am Legend* are represented as non-human or sub-human monsters. In Math-eson's novel and in *The Last Man on Earth*, Neville/Morgan discovers at the end that he has been killing both mindless revenant vampires *and* conscious living vampires. As a result, he becomes the freak for the reader/viewer if not for himself – he is the murderous boogieman who comes in the day to murder sleeping vampires. In *The Last Man on Earth*, *The Omega Man* and *Rabid* – as in virtually every other vampire movie in which normal human beings are infected and 'turned' – the vampires are infected human beings. In contrast, in *I Am Legend*, those infected with the vampirism virus are transformed into savage beasts with heightened physical abilities but diminished cognitive ones. They are, in essence, animalised. In this way, *I Am Legend* carefully avoids anything that might call into question the ethi-cal stance of its hero, Neville, as he fends off these monsters and works to cure or kill them – or I should say *almost* anything.

It is true that Robert does not spend his time mass-producing stakes with a lathe and picking off vampires in their sleep, as does Neville in the novel. Neville in *I Am Legend*, the always-likeable Will Smith, doesn't seek a fight, and when it comes, he fights monsters for whom the viewer can have little sympathy, rather than identifiably human beings. Where the film, however, does raise issues concerning Robert's ethics is over his use of captured vampires as guinea pigs in his quest to find a cure for the vampire plague. Robert, who was a US army virologist, has converted the basement of his Washington Square townhouse bunker into a medical facility and spends his days developing vaccines that he then injects into his conscripted subjects. The viewer learns through photographs on his walls that Neville's attempts to develop a cure have failed many, many times – resulting in the deaths of many, many vampire subjects. Neville himself has no qualms about his use of live subjects, but the look of dismay on Anna's (Alice Braga) face as she surveys the photographs of Neville's failures effectively raises questions concerning Neville's ethics for the audience, if not for him.

I Am Legend is thus a vampire film organised around contemporary anxieties concerning science and it illustrates clearly the inherent connection between the vampire cinema and the theme of the human relationship to technology. It is a film in which the quest for a cancer vaccine creates a disease that transforms people into monsters. The hero, Robert Neville, is a scientist who continues to perform medical experiments seeking to understand what went wrong and to develop a cure. By experimenting on live vampire subjects, Neville's actions not only tap into anxieties about the unintended or unforeseen consequences of scientific experimentation but obliquely raise concerns about the ethics of vivisection – questions are raised about Neville's use of live subjects for his experiments even if the film ultimately validates his actions as necessary to the perpetuation of the human race. Medical technology thus produces both the vampire as epidemic and the cure; *I Am Legend* illustrates both the peril and promise of science and, as with *The Last Man on Earth* and *Rabid*, taps into deepseated cultural anxieties about the ways in which science is conducted and utilised.

Guns, Germs and Silver: The Action Vampire Movie

The films above redefine the vampire as a 'natural' entity produced by natural forces. In *The Last Man on Earth*, *Rabid* and *I Am Legend*, vampirism is the lamentable consequence of science outstripping reason and/or human control. The exact cause of vampirism in *The Last Man on Earth* isn't revealed, but Matheson's novel implies that it was nuclear war or germ warfare. In *Rabid*, vampirism is caused by the experimental grafting of embryonic stem cells. In *I Am Legend*, even benevolent science is suspect as the source of the vampire plague is a newly developed cure for cancer. In each case, the vampire is the product of technological intervention into nature. Interestingly, in these films human beings *become* vampires through the scientific manipulation of the environment. Each of these three movies thus offers a cautionary tale about the use and abuse of science.

But science holds possibility as well as peril and this exciting aspect of science is emphasised most vividly in what I call the action vampire movie – films such as *Van Helsing*, the *Blade* series and the *Underworld* series that are less horror movies than action movies in which ultra-sexy protagonists contend against dangerous (and sexy) vampire opponents in scenes of carefully choreographed violence and spectacular special effects. What these films make apparent in a very explicit manner is that vampire films have always been on some level about toys and tools – that is, about the devices that one finds or develops to combat the vampire. The repertoire of vampire prophylactics and eradicants has remained fairly consistent across the genre. In *Dracula* (1931), garlic, crosses and stakes do the trick. Sunlight as a potent force is harnessed in films from *Nosferatu* (1922) to *I Am Legend*. Occasionally, other tools are employed, such as the hawthorn branch that participates in doing in Dracula in *The Satanic Rites of Dracula* (1974). But although the methods have remained fairly consistent, the means of delivery have changed with the times and have become increasingly sophisticated. To illustrate this point, I will focus briefly on the *Blade* films (reserving an expanded discussion of *Blade* for Chapter Three) and more fully on the most visible example of this phenomenon, *Van Helsing* from 2004, starring Hugh Jackman and Kate Beckinsale.

The Blade Franchise
Blade, which was released in 1998 and is loosely based on the Marvel Comics half man/half vampire hero of the same name, is the film most fully responsible for initiating the recent cycle of big-budget vampire action movies (the *Underworld* films, the very interesting *Night Watch* films (*Night Watch* (2004), *Day Watch* (2006)), the videogame-based *BloodRayne* films (*BloodRayne* (2006), *BloodRayne II: Deliverance* (2007)), the barely mediocre *Van Helsing*, *Ultraviolet* (2006), *30 Days of Night*, and so forth) through

its infusion of 'an MTV aesthetic and ample doses of flamboyant violence' (Prince 2004: 1). *Blade* was far from being the first vampire film to incorporate choreographed martial arts sequences – attempting to capitalise on the popularity of Bruce Lee kung fu movies, Hammer Studios released *The Legend of the 7 Golden Vampires* in 1974, and the 1980s witnessed a series of vampire/kung fu hybrid films from Asia including *Encounters of the Spooky Kind* (1980) and the Hong Kong *Mr Vampire* series that began in 1986. Nor was *Blade* the first shoot-'em-up action vampire film – a distinction that arguably goes to Robert Rodriguez's *From Dusk Till Dawn* in 1996, although there are plenty of guns in *Near Dark* and *Innocent Blood*, and the related vampire/western synthesis can be traced back to the forgettable *Curse of the Undead* (1959) and the ridiculous *Billy the Kid vs. Dracula* starring an aged John Carradine. But what *Blade* did was to fuse effectively the action movie appeal of the popular *Lethal Weapon* (beginning in 1987) and *Die Hard* (beginning in 1988) series with a comic book ethos of *Batman* (1989) and to electrify the hybrid with a hipper-than-thou attitude and ultra-cool aesthetic.

Blade, it is fair to say, is up-to-date with a vengeance and works to establish its edgy, hip ambience from the very first scene in which a hapless human victim is taken to a vampire 'blood rave' at a slaughter house by his vampire pick-up who, following in Marilyn Chambers' footsteps in *Rabid*, is played by notorious porn star Traci Lords (who created a cause célèbre when it was revealed that much of her work was done before she was the legal age of eighteen). The true spectacle at the rave, however, is not the rain of blood that cascades from the fire extinguishers to the pulsating beat of New Order but the intervention of Blade himself, the 'day walker' (Wesley Snipes), whose sculpted, sunglasses-clad, hyperbolically-masculine form moves confidently through the panicked vampire crowd wreaking havoc with both modern and modernised archaic weapons – guns that fire silver bullets and a silver sword (modified to accept only his grip) that reduce vampires instantly to cinders.

What the viewer discovers is that Blade is both hybrid and cyborg – he is half vampire/half human (hence his ability to tolerate daylight), and he technologically suppresses his thirst for blood with periodic injections of a serum (recalling the blood substitute consumed by the vampire-heroine Vampirella in the film of the same name from 1996) developed by his mentor, weapons designer and substitute father, Abraham Whistler (Kris

Kristofferson). In the relative safety of their industrial park compound, Whistler operates a workshop in which he develops sophisticated anti-vampire weaponry. Upping the technology quotient of the film is Dr Karen Jenson (N'Bushe Wright), a vampire-bite victim who coincidentally happens to be a haematologist. Karen, searching for a cure for the vampirism 'virus', discovers that an anticoagulant called EDTA reacts violently with vampire blood cells – a weapon that comes in handy later in the film when Blade confronts the film's villain, upstart 'turned' vampire Deacon Frost (Stephen Dorff), who has acquired super powers (even by vampire standards) through an ancient ritual.

At the heart of *Blade* is both a discourse about race (to be discussed in Chapter Three) and a discourse about technology and the pace of technological change. Blade represents a new breed of vampire hunter with science on his side who comes equipped with increasingly sophisticated tools at his disposal. He uses advanced technology both to control his own vampiric thirst and to pursue his quarry. Simultaneously, Dr Jenson puts her technological expertise to use developing a medical cure for vampirism. For his part, Frost is able to assume supremacy over the 'pure blood' vampire elders through his use of computers whose data processing abilities allow him to unlock ancient vampire secrets. The vampire elders in *Blade* are behind the times and wed to the 'old ways', which result in their downfall. Both Blade and Frost utilise modern technology to achieve their objectives and the Blade versus Frost contest thus constitutes a showdown between good science and bad science.

This theme of good science versus bad science is developed even more fully in *Blade II*, directed by Guillermo del Toro (who also directed *Cronos*, discussed below), in which Blade must join forces with a team of vampires called the Bloodpack trained as assassins (with the original intention of battling Blade himself) to track down and kill a genetic mutation – a ravenous vampiric creature called a Reaper that feeds on both humans and vampires and whose viral bite is so infectious that victims turn into Reapers almost immediately after being bitten. In the process of combating the Reapers, Whistler, joined by assistant Scud (Norman Reedus), develops an ultraviolet light grenade, a remote-controlled explosive that implants in one character's head, machineguns that shoot silver bullets, and other devices. But the real twist of the film is that the Reapers turn out to be the product of conscious genetic engineering on the part of vampire elder, Eli Damaskinos

(Thomas Kretschmann), who is intent upon creating a superior race of vampires that lacks the typical vampire weaknesses. Jared Nomak (Luke Goss) the first Reaper and carrier of the Reaper virus (*Blade II*'s 'Typhoid Mary') is thus Damoskinos's genetically engineered son – who kills his father in the end for his hubris.

The third film in the *Blade* trilogy, *Blade: Trinity*, does an interesting twist on the infection vampire movie theme by introducing a virus that doesn't turn people into vampires, but rather that will wipe out the world's population of vampires. Indeed, this is a film that pits two possible genocidal outcomes against each other, but that – with uninterrogated ethical implications – rejects one while easily accepting the other. With clear reference to Nazi Germany's planning and execution of systematic genocide against European Jewry in World War II, the vampires in *Blade: Trinity* are attempting to develop what is referred to as the 'vampire final solution', a reinvigoration of their debased bloodline through an infusion of pure blood right from the source – the original Dracula – that will allow them to walk in daylight and thus enslave all humanity. Also revealed in the film is that the vampires have developed blood 'farming' facilities in which – with interesting connections to the *Matrix* films (which the film in fact explicitly acknowledges when it has heroine Abigail Whistler (Jessica Biel) provoke her opponent with the beckoning hand summons made famous by the character Morpheus (Laurence Fishburne) from *The Matrix*) – homeless people are rounded up and kept in chemically-induced comas in a giant *X-Files*-esque warehouse while their blood is harvested (a scenario that appears borrowed from *Thirst* (1979)). To combat this vampire scourge, the forces of good in *Blade: Trinity* develop their own genocidal programme to counter that of the vampires. They engineer a virus called 'Daystar' which, when combined with Dracula's blood, will become a global pandemic eradicating all vampires. At the end of the film this seems to be precisely what has occurred.

The three *Blade* films represent a remarkable concatenation of modern anxieties and fantasies about science. All three revel in the technological sublimity of advanced weaponry – weapons of light and silver that leave behind only dust in their wake as vampires are endlessly and mechanically dispatched. But all three also tap into deep-seated anxieties about the destructive potential of science as vampires and vampire hunters engage in what can only be described as an arms race involving genetic engineering and germ warfare. In the end, the humans develop their own 'final solution', the Daystar virus that wipes out all the vampires, including the original vampire, Dracula, tellingly resurrected (as noted in the Introduction to this book) from his tomb in Iraq. The half-human Blade survives, but one wonders what his place and purpose will be in a world without vampires to battle. More disconcerting are the questions the film never stops to ask – questions about the ethics of wiping out an entire species that, according to the film, has existed for over 5,000 years; questions about the impact on the environment of making vampires extinct; and questions about the possible implications of releasing an untested, experimental engineered virus into the atmosphere. The true 'blade' in these films is science – and what the vampire genre shows us again and again is that it is a double-edged sword.

Van Helsing

Science in *Van Helsing* is clearly presented as just such a double-edged sword, if alas a dull one. *Van Helsing* indeed is interesting not so much for what it originates, as for what it appropriates. The film (like the equally ridiculous *The League of Extraordinary Gentlemen* which came out one year before *Van Helsing* and fascinatingly features the character Mina Harker (Peta Wilson) as an unapologetic vampire) is a postmodern patchwork quilt composed of threads taken from a variety of novels and other movies. Despite boasting the talents of Hugh Jackman playing the title role of Abraham Van Helsing and Kate Beckinsale as his potential love interest, the film has trouble rising above its absurd plot, poor writing, poorer accents and, in general, so much tortured effort to be cool that it degenerates quickly into camp. Nonetheless, as a James Bond-meets-Dracula pastiche, it vividly illustrates the contemporary action vampire movie trend in which technology itself takes centre stage.

In brief, Dracula needs the Frankenstein monster as a sort of living battery to vivify his monstrous progeny, which are born simply dead rather than undead. Abraham Van Helsing – who it appears is also the Archangel Gabriel but can't remember it (angels apparently being prone to amnesia) – is there to stop him, which can only be accomplished by Van Helsing transforming into a werewolf (angels apparently being susceptible to werewolf venom).

Both in terms of style and content, technology is the movie's real star. On the level of style, the film – directed by Stephen Sommers who also directed the *Mummy* films with Brendan Fraser starting in 1990 – is clearly in love with computer-generated special effects. After contending with the wholly CGI generated Mr Hyde (appropriated wholesale, it seems, from *The League of Extraordinary Gentleman* in which Hyde becomes an important player and, bizarrely, a force for good), Van Helsing must face Dracula's brides as they swoop from the sky and transform from harpies into exotically-garbed seductresses in the blink of an eye and who, *Blade*-like, turn instantly to dust when staked through the heart. As the film progresses, men transform into werewolves and vice versa; Dracula takes an Escher-esque walk on the ceiling; and all of the major characters perform a variety of physically-implausible or down-right impossible feats of derring-do. Indeed, the body itself is reconceived as plastic and malleable in *Van Helsing* – something to be stretched and transformed through the use of special effects.

Yet beyond the CGI love affair of the film in which not only the vampires but all the characters are constructed and transformed by special effects, technology itself becomes a conscious theme of the film. Part of the vampire movie formula, as mentioned above, is determining how to combat the vampire and equipping oneself with the necessary tools to do the job. The vampire genre thus implies a certain level of technological sophistication. *Van Helsing* however highlights this aspect of the formula and takes it to parodic levels. Van Helsing, one discovers early on, is a monster hunter working for a secret organisation called the Knights of the Holy Order that operates a James Bond-like laboratory in a hidden compound beneath the Vatican. Here a surprisingly (and none-too-convincingly) multicultural and pan-religious assortment of scientists and craftspeople, including Friar Carl, the film's bumbling Q stand-in, develop various weapons to combat evil. In a scene taken straight from the James Bond films (and parodied by the *Austin Powers* films (1997, 1999, 2002)), Carl walks Van Helsing through the laboratory, demonstrating several of the dangerous tools in development before equipping Van Helsing with a repeating crossbow with a magazine of bolts and showing him a 'light bomb' (ripped off from *Blade II*) that can emit a burst of light as brilliant as the sun. Both devices, in keeping with the principle of 'Chekov's gun' which states that any object introduced early in the plot must be used later on (and that important objects utilised later on must have been introduced earlier), come in handy along the way in dealing with Dracula, his body-suited green-screened vampire brides, and his host of vampire followers who gather at an All Hallow's Eve masquerade ball. The film, much like *Blade* and *Blade II* from which it borrows freely, thus consciously delights in the technological aspect of the vampire movie, turning the conventional process of determining how to kill the vampire into a carnival with a cabinet of wonders at its centre.

The vampire, as in both *Blade* and *Blade II*, of course has his own scientific agenda in *Van Helsing* and here is where the film intersects with issues surrounding modern technology in a different way as it – like *Blade II* – interestingly seems informed by contemporary debates over reproductive technology and genetic manipulation. Not only does Dracula appear to be a chemist who has developed a formula that can cure lycanthropy (since Dracula in this film – as is developed in the *Underworld* series – uses werewolf labour despite the fact that he can only be killed by a werewolf, he needs a way to 'cure' them if they get out of hand), but we discover that he in fact commissioned and financed the construction of Frankenstein's monster because he needs him as a kind of electrical conduit to energise his thousands of baby vampire-ettes. Dracula and his three wives want nothing more than to raise a family – albeit a non-traditional one – and the typical mode of vampire family creation, adoption through 'turning', is for some reason unsatisfactory. So they need a sort of surrogate mother in Frankenstein's monster who will provide the necessary amniotic juice needed to shock the kids into undeadness.

What I find interesting here – and what links *Van Helsing* not only with the *Blade* films but with the infection vampire films as well – is that *Van Helsing* is yet another vampire movie that embeds anxieties about 'unnatural' propagation, reproductive technologies and genetic manipulation. Dracula in this film is in essence a mad scientist intent on designing an 'unnatural' counter-normative family. His 'bad science' must be countered by the good science of the Knights of the Holy Order who send their representative Van Helsing, armed with anachronistic ballistic inventions, precisely to protect the traditional *family* – the viewer learns that the good Valerius family has been hampered by an ancestor's vow that no member of the family will go to heaven until Dracula is dead and now several generations are waiting in limbo, presumably rooting for the last members of their family line, Anna (Beckinsale) and Velkan (Will Kemp), to finish the job. *Van Helsing* is ultimately an extremely conservative 'family values' film that reaffirms the sanctity of the traditional nuclear family and that – like *Blade II* – glamourises weaponry and 'defense spending' while demonising (more or less literally) technologies that facilitate reproduction outside of the conventional family unit.

A Date With Dracula: Bram Stoker's Dracula

Having considered the ways in which the cinematic vampire is always a cyborg, always related to and produced by technologies of detection, definition and destruction, and always defined in relation to science, I now wish to consider the issue of the vampire cinema from a different perspective. My argument here is that our thinking about the cinema itself has been influenced by the idea of vampirism. Before moving back in time to the beginnings of cinema itself and then working my way forward, I will start with a late twentieth-century movie that provocatively thematises the vampire's relationship to cinema: Francis Ford Coppola's *Bram Stoker's Dracula*. From there, I will jump back in time to consider two early vampire films, *Nosferatu* and *Vampyr*, that demonstrate the connection between the vampire and cinematic effects before moving forward again to *The Shadow of the Vampire*, the film that most explicitly establishes the parallel between cinema and vampirism.

Bram Stoker's Dracula is a movie that is intensely cinematic – that is, it is one that through its conspicuous use of special effects and cinematic 'tricks', self-referentially calls attention to its own status as a movie. It is a film that, on one level, is thus all about movies and movie making – and one that throughout links everyone's favourite vampire, played by Gary Oldman, to the cinema. Among the many scenes in the film that, despite the movie's assertive title, do *not* appear in Stoker's book, two back-to-back ones stand out for our purposes: the ones in which Count Dracula and Mina Murray (Winona Ryder) take in a movie.

The first of these scenes opens with an effect that perhaps more explicitly than any other scene in the film self-referentially foregrounds the celluloid nature of the cinematic text the viewer is watching as it is made to appear as if the circular iris of an antique camera is opening onto a sepia-toned street scene. In the background is heard the sound of a projector, furthering the impression that the viewer is watching a silent film. The motion of the camera as it descends from above to street level is jerky and the movements of the horse-drawn carriages and Victorian-garbed pedestrians are mechanical and sped up, as if the product of an under-cranked camera.

All of this creates the impression of 'vintageness' and indeed the beginning of the sequence was shot with a turn-of-the-century hand-cranked Pathé camera owned by Coppola. This is modern cinema masquerading as antique cinema.

Represented in the scene is Count Dracula moving about during the day (which, it is worth mentioning, he does in Stoker's novel as well – the vampire's 'allergy' to sunlight, as Peter Cushing's Van Helsing in *The Horror of Dracula* puts it, is a later invention), and what the viewer discovers is that the Count's arrival in London has been made to coincide with the introduction of the Lumière brothers' 'amazing Cinematograph' – which the Count uses as a convenient way to break the ice with his reincarnated lost love, Mina (a subplot that also is *not* in Stoker's novel), as he asks her for directions to what he has heard is the 'wonder of the civilised world'. After some perfunctory indignation on Mina's part (and stilted acting on Ryder's) over being approached by a stranger on the street, she consents to show the Count the way (how she knows the way isn't revealed – has she already seen the film?). Dracula and Mina's first date thus is a trip to the movies.

As Johan Callens observes, this scene in which the Count is tracked on the street and appears as a character in an early twentieth-century silent movie already serves to connect the Count with the medium of cinema

Bram Stoker's Dracula: The Count at the movies

(2006: 199), and this identification is emphasised further when the Count is impressed by the spectacle of the film they view, a Lumière brothers-esque shot of a train arriving, commenting ironically, 'Astounding. There are no limits to science.' Here is where things get really interesting. In actuality, four silent film sequences are included in the background of this scene. The first which introduces the scene at the movies – even before the arriving train – features the 'stop trick' or substitution effect pioneered by Georges Méliès in 1896. In this brief sequence, a middle-aged man invites two attractive and scantily-clad young women onto his lap only to have them suddenly transform, much to the man's displeasure, into a more matronly apron-clad older woman who is shooed off the man's lap. The second silent movie snippet, which appears to be an altered and/or staged version of the Lumière brothers' *L'Arrivée d'un train en Gare de la Ciotat* (1895), shows an approaching train moving across a desolate landscape. The third, which is glimpsed briefly as the Count has pinned Mina down on a sort of sofa or divan compelling her to recognise him, features a naked woman of the Theda Bara vamp school who turns and walks away from the camera. And the final silent film snippet, which shifts back to the style of Méliès, shows an upright woman standing in a coffin who transforms into a skeleton before the viewer's eyes and is visible at the moment that the Count has restrained himself from biting Mina (and that an escaped wolf makes its appearance in the theatre precipitating some literal heavy petting on the part of the Count and Mina, leather gloves not withstanding).

The four silent movie snippets, it is worth noting, create a compelling (and interestingly misogynistic) mini-narrative on their own: as with Jonathan Harker, a man is first attracted to and then repelled by transforming women; reversing the course of the train that carries Jonathan Harker east earlier in the film, the Count, who is clearly paralleled with the train later in the scene, arrives in London; another seduction takes place; and death ensues. Beyond this, however, the fleeting juxtaposition of the realistic scene of a train arriving with the morbidly surreal scene of a woman departing (or at least transforming) highlights the artificial and phantasmatic core of cinema itself. Replicating the familiar dualistic assessment of the Lumière brothers as proto-realists and Méliès as the progenitor of the surreal, the train, one could argue, at first glance appears to carry us out of the world we know and into a world of fantasy and horror; however, what the 'stagey-ness' of the film within a film foregrounds is that the train is no more 'real' than the women's transformations. The difference between the two is that the Méliès-esque snippet makes use of rudimentary special effects that violate what we have come to appreciate as realism while the Lumière brothers' snippet corresponds to what we have come to associate with realism. Neither is 'real'.

Even within a movie that is quite consciously cinematic, the scene at the Cinematograph is the moment at which the film turns back upon itself most vividly, emphasising both the cinematic nature of the vampire and the vampiric nature of cinema. In mobius strip-like fashion, a modern film stages a Victorian scene and is shot using antiquated equipment; the scene then transforms into one shot using modern equipment and conforming to the conventions of modern cinema, but that incorporates faux antique film footage. All four films within the film additionally capture a moment in time that is endlessly repeated (the train arriving scene is shown at least three times in the background) freezing the phantasmatic projections of their referents in an uncanny limbo space between presence and absence, life and death.

And at the centre of this movie about the making of movies and the artifice of movies is the vampire, Count Dracula, who himself becomes associated with the technology used to make movies most explicitly when, during the second repetition of the train arriving scene, he appears backed by the screen, a projection overlapping a projection, his cane at one point splitting the screen behind him and obscuring the approaching train. Dracula here, as Stacey Abbott (2007) asserts, is not (or not just) the atavistic emergence of some archaic force, but rather a force of modernity itself. He, not the Crew of Light (to borrow Christopher Craft's term) that pursues him, is the one fascinated with modern technology. While they go backward in time to crosses and communion wafers, it is our vampire – himself a creature of 'special effects' who can transform himself in various ways – who is looking ahead in time, amazed by the miracles of modern science. What Coppola's film shows us is the vampire present at the birth of modern cinema and the correspondence between the two – each creating legions of the undead.

Having seen the vampire present at and appreciative of the birth of cinema in Coppola's movie, we will now time travel ourselves, going back briefly to the origins of cinema in which filmmakers including Georges Méliès and the Lumière brothers pioneered cinema's uncanny ability to preserve and manipulate images, before moving forward in time again to consider three films that illustrate the 'vampire cinema' – the vampire as cinematic and the cinema as vampiric.

Between Life and Death: George Méliès

The cinema can be perceived as and compared to an uncanny medium – a force that conjures phantoms and preserves the dead, even as it drains the life out of the living. Lloyd Michaels notes this supernatural quality of cinema when he observes the ways in which film both deceives and enthralls the spectator 'by substituting an illusory presence for an absent referent, rendering as "undead" a lost object by animating projected shadows and light' (1998: 238). Cinema, through the manipulation of light and shadow, conjures into being the phantasmatic half-presence of something absent. The screen is thus populated by ghosts – the uncanny, endlessly repeated afterlife of the absent people and objects represented. Expressing a similar sentiment in a more vampiric register, Abbott writes, 'Made up of still images, ghostly shadows of the dead that are reanimated through technological means, film bears striking parallels with vampirism' (2007: 43), and then goes on to speak about the turn-of-the-nineteenth-century 'technological necromancy' (2007: 44) of the camera, the gramophone, the X-ray, and even of electricity that allowed ephemeral and insubstantial phenomena such as light and sound and electrons to be captured and transformed.

Abbott's point here is that, developing out of the traditions of the Phantasmagoria, a form of magic lantern projecting ghostly shadows, and what was known as Pepper's Ghost, an illusionary technique using glass that would allow actors to seem to appear and disappear or morph into other shapes, modern cinema was preoccupied from its very beginnings with the fantastic and surreal. Perhaps the first to realise and harness the potential uncanniness of the cinematic medium was French cinema pioneer Georges Méliès, sometimes referred to as the 'Cinemagician', who is credited with having invented horror cinema. As the delightful story goes, Méliès, a former stage magician, accidentally discovered the 'stop trick', or substitution (basically, stopping the camera and substituting one object for another, thus making it appear that one object has turned into another), in 1896 when his camera jammed while filming street traffic in Paris. When he viewed the footage later, an omnibus had 'magically' turned into a hearse.

This transformation – and the potential the cinema held for others – spurred Méliès' early interest in 'exploring the "supernatural" capacities of the moving picture' (Jacobs 1968: 23). In addition to the stop trick, he was one of the first filmmakers to incorporate time-lapse photography, multiple exposures, dissolves and hand-painted colours.

Although the story about Méliès' camera 'accidentally' jamming on the Parisian streets may well be apocryphal (see Michaels 1998), the result is too perfect for this study to resist and illustrates my contention about the vampiric nature of cinema itself: one of cinema's earliest creations dramatises the transformation of life into death as an omnibus metamorphoses into a hearse and then repeats (or re-hearses) that narrative endlessly! And it is the camera here that has sucked the life out of the omnibus passengers, rendering them 'dead', only then continually to animate and kill them again and again. As Abbott notes, the cinema's first filmmakers, including Méliès whose early films were suffused with magical and supernatural themes and images, inherited from photography and magic lantern shows not only a technical language but also a 'preoccupation with the fantastic as a means of showcasing the spectral nature of film', concluding that 'the exploration of the potential for film and the development of more elabourate fantasy narratives went hand in hand' as Méliès and other filmmakers explored and mastered cinema's potential (2007: 50). There was something uncanny about film from the start.

Nosferatu: Count Orlok's Shadow

Georges Méliès has been credited with being the father of horror cinema and although most famous for his *Le voyage dans la lune* (1902), many of his productions such as *Le Manior du Diable* (1896), *Le Monstre* (1903), *Le Chaudron Infernal* (1903), *Le Diable* (1905), and others do indeed introduce a panoply of stock Gothic features including dancing skeletons, the devil, witches, ghosts and what has been described as the cinema's first vampire – a devilish fellow in *Le Manior du Diable* who is warded off with a large cross. Equally magical, however, during film's first decades was the developing technology and sophistication of filmmaking. Sabine Hake writes that pre-World War I German cinema was marked by a kind of conscious self-referentiality intended to 'show audiences how to appreciate the cinema and its increasingly sophisticated products, how to deal with feelings of astonishment and disbelief, and how to gain satisfaction from the playful awareness of the apparatus and the simultaneous denial of its presence' (1996: 237–8). Cinema as conjuration was a new experience at the turn of the twentieth century and audience members had to be schooled concerning how to watch movies – to develop a sort of double-consciousness (that we today take for granted) that allows one to recognise the film as artifice while simultaneously suspending one's disbelief (or at least allowing oneself to be seduced and captivated by narrative). Early cinema had to create its audience, so to speak – spectators who could enjoy, rather than faint at, the sight of a train heading for them, the devil appearing out of nowhere, or the vampire rising stiffly from his coffin.

The self-referentiality of pre-World War I German cinema was only amplified in post-World War I German cinematic expressionism that utilised stylistic and special effects to distort reality for emotional impact. The acknowledged master of combining technical virtuosity with romantic narrative was F. W. Murnau, director of what remains one of the most significant films in the vampire cinema tradition, *Nosferatu*. According to Lotte H. Eisner, Murnau was the greatest filmmaker Germany has ever known (1973: 97) and his cinematic innovations in *Nosferatu* are well documented. What is particularly interesting for our purposes here however, is that, as Abbott observes, drawing upon the work of film historian David Skal, the relationship between the vampire and film itself was part of the film's earliest conception. Abbott asserts that '*Nosferatu* imbues its vampire with the filmic and photographic qualities of the cinema as a means of exploring the inherent vampirism of this new technology' (2007: 52). Thus, when the film's Jonathan Harker character, Hutter (Gustav von Wangenheim), crosses over into the realm of the vampire, 'the land of phantoms', Murnau employs a negative shot that creates a ghostly world of shadows. When Count Orlok's coach arrives for Hutter, Murnau undercranks the camera to create the effect of 'fast motion' (Abbott 2007: 54). Orlok (Max Schreck) again is filmed in fast motion when he loads his dirt-filled coffins onto a cart and stop-motion is used to create the effect of the lid of the coffin magically moving into place. When Orlok reveals himself for what he is, a vampire, superimposition (double exposure) is used to create an uncanny effect (Orlok essentially 'fades out' in one place only to 'fade in' in another). For Michaels, these effects illustrate the 'affinity between the cinema's process of signification involving the play of presence/absence' and the vampire's 'elusive existence' (1998: 242; 248). Lane Roth similarly observes the ways in which these techniques emphasise the role of the camera as a 'seeing subject, as shaper of perception' (1984: 247). The vampire himself is a 'special effect' of cinema. Nowhere is this connection made more explicit than through the film's famous use of shadow.

Nosferatu, as both Eisner and Skal comment, is filled with striking images – the most striking of which are associated with the vampire, Count Orlok. Orlok's first appearance as he emerges from darkness to meet Hutter; his staring at Ellen (the film's Mina Harker, played by Greta Schröder) from behind the bars of his window in Wisborg 'clinging to a window grid like a spider in a Bauhaus web' (Skal 2004: 87); and his clutching his heart before disappearing in a puff of smoke at the end all are triumphs of framing and composition. The film's most memorable image, however, arguably is that of the vampire's shadow creeping up the stairs to Ellen's room, grotesque hands stretching and elongating toward the door. Murnau, as has often been noted, diverged from the expressionist filmmakers of his era through the innovative decision for the time to film on location, including out of doors. Nonetheless, these striking images, masterpieces of chiaroscuro, clearly participate in the expressionistic tradition. And, beyond this, the

Nosferatu: Murnau's expressionistic use of shadow

vampire as a creature of shadow further develops the connection between the vampire and cinema – Orlok's shadow, as Abbott notes, is projected like film onto white surfaces, partaking of film's 'shadowy nature' (2007: 52–3).

Count Orlok in *Nosferatu* is thus a creature of light, shadow and cinematic trickery – which is to say that he is a technological invention. A fabrication of cinema's manipulation of images, the vampire has no corresponding real world referent. He is purely and properly cinematic. But what *Nosferatu* also makes clear are the parallels between the vampire and the cinema itself – a central focus of *Shadow of the Vampire*, which I will turn to in a moment. Before doing so, however, I would like to attend to one other early twentieth century vampire movie that also constructs for us the technological vampire – the vampire as a cinematic entity fashioned by cinematic magic, Carl-Theodor Dreyer's *Vampyr*.

Vampyr – Vampire Space

Vampyr has a vampire in it; but apart from that, it bears little resemblance to any other film in this study. A summary of the plot only starts to suggest the unusual nature of the film: protagonist Allan Grey (Julian West), a young man of undetermined background and profession, checks into a hotel near the French town of Courtempierre. After running into several odd characters in the strangely labyrinthine hotel, he is confronted in his room by an elderly man (Maurice Schutz) who tells him that 'she must not die!' and presents him with wrapped package of some kind, instructing Grey that it should only be opened upon his death. Grey starts snooping around and discovers something that seems borrowed from Murnau's *Nosferatu*: shadows that move on their own without anything to cast them – the shadow of a man digging a hole, the shadow of a man with a wooden leg, small dancing shadows. Allan hears dogs barking and a child crying and he runs into the village Doctor (Jan Heironimko), who tells him that there are neither dogs nor children at the hotel. After Allan leaves him, the doctor is given a bottle of poison by an old woman.

Already strange, things take a particularly surreal turn as Allan follows dancing shadows to a nearby chateau occupied by the old man who gave him the package and his two daughters, Gisèlle (Rena Handel) and Léone (Sybille Schmitz). They are awaiting the arrival of the doctor because Léone is ill. Abruptly, the old man is killed – apparently by a gun-toting shadow – and Allan is asked to stay with the family while a servant goes by coach for the police. While he waits, Allan opens the mysterious package to discover a book entitled 'The History of Vampires' (*Vampyr*'s version of *Nosferatu's* 'Book of the Vampires'), which he starts to read.

His reading is interrupted by Gisèlle, who spies Léone moving through the yard. Allan and Gisèlle go after her and discover her prostrate form. The coach returns, bearing the body of the murdered coachman, and once Léone is back inside, she is seized by blood-lust and appears poised to attack her sister when she is interrupted by the entrance of a nurse. Meanwhile, Allan continues to read 'The History of Vampires', which provides a parallel narrative to the one the viewer is watching as it explains, among other things, that vampires command the shadows of executed criminals and tells the story of a vampire woman named Marguerite Chopin assisted by a village doctor. The village doctor at this point arrives to tend to Léone and determines that she needs blood, which Allan is conscripted to provide. While Allan is resting after having given blood, one of the servants reads from the book.

Allan is awoken from a dream just in time to prevent Léone from drinking poison left behind by the doctor who flees, taking Gisèlle as a prisoner. (Vampires, 'The History of Vampires' reveals, attempt to drive their victims to commit suicide, which is a mortal sin and delivers the victims over to the dark side. The question of whether or not drinking poison by accident counts as suicide is not one engaged by the film.) Allan goes after the doctor, but collapses and in what is arguably the film's most famous sequence, his shadow or spirit separates from his body and goes to the doctor's house where he discovers Gisèlle tied up and his own body in a coffin. The point of view shifts to within the coffin and Allan observes what transpires through a small window as the coffin is nailed shut and carried to the cemetery. He is to be buried alive!

Allan awakens from his reverie – or his spirit rejoins his body – and he proceeds to the cemetery with the same servant who has read from 'The History of Vampires'. They open the grave of a woman named Marguerite Chopin (the same woman apparently who is specifically mentioned in 'The History of Vampires') and the servant drives a stake through her heart. The curse on Gisèlle and Léone is lifted. The doctor and his peg-legged assistant are now haunted by the ghost of the murdered father whose over-sized face appears flashing in a window. The assistant dies of unexplained causes and the doctor is chased to a flour mill where the servant who dispatched the vampire now suffocates the doctor under a mountain of flour.

As this synopsis suggests, *Vampyr* is a very different vampire film from Tod Browning's *Dracula* – the famous version with Bela Lugosi – that was produced at the same time, although released one year earlier in 1931. There are no suave aristocratic vampires in top hats here! And our ostensible 'hero', Allan Grey, is curiously inert – doing little more than observing events rather than actively intervening. He does not identify or dispatch the vampire. But the differences – and difficulties – of *Vampyr* are not simply plot-related. Indeed, my summation of the plot makes it seem far more coherent and readily intelligible than it actually is. Instead, as David Bordwell has developed at length in his excellent study of Dreyer, the film constantly works to retard conclusions and obfuscate meaning. 'Consequences are shown', writes Bordwell, 'but causes are concealed', creating a film in which 'the principal story becomes half-hidden, as obscure as the misty landscapes throughout the film' (1981: 94; 96). *Vampyr* is a vampire movie that defamiliarises or 'makes strange' both the world it represents and the process of watching movies. One struggles to make sense of what is happening, to relate causes to effects, to organise the disparate scenes and sequences into a coherent narrative. The film itself in a sense is 'supernatural', one that highlights the uncanniness of film itself.

Bordwell's careful analysis reveals the ways in which the film's artistic arrangement of events – the plot – works together with the film's formal elements – its filming and editing – to create a dense, shadowy work full of 'snares and bafflements' (1981: 116). He notes that cause-effect relations are undone by what he refers to as 'ellipsis', 'retardation' and 'viewpoint'. Cross-cutting fragments narrative continuity creating 'elliptical' narrative sequences. Unanswered and unanswerable questions are introduced, diverting the viewer and retarding the drawing of conclusions. And restricting point of view to a single perspective (usually – but not always – Allan Gray) 'makes what occurs outside that ken somewhat uncertain and ambiguous ... Making Gray the protagonist makes gray the story' (1981: 97).

Beyond these devices, however, Bordwell emphasises the ways in which the filming of *Vampyr* reorganises space in confusing ways. 'In *Vampyr*, space is fluid, plastic, uncertain; its unfolding foils and baffles us; the revelation of space, rather than situating us more comfortably, disorients us'

(1981: 98). Lighting in the film, as has frequently been remarked, leaves objects and locations misty and undefined. Famously, Dreyer filmed outdoor shots with a veil over the camera to create a sense of fog and indistinctness (see Jones 2002: 92). For David Pirie, this creates an atmosphere of 'miasmic horror' (1977: 47). For Bordwell, this diffusion of light in a sense dematerialises objects, flattening them and questioning their solidity. Camera movement as well complicates and interrupts any construction of continuous space and concrete on- and off-screen reality.

The world of *Vampyr* is thus one in which shadows move on their own accord and in which the camera becomes an 'independent factor' foregrounding 'the active role of the camera in constituting and questioning cinematic space' and dismantling the 'phenomenal continuum of traditional cinematic representation' (Bordwell 1981: 105; 108). As such, *Vampyr*, even more so than *Nosferatu*, is what I call an intensely cinematic film, and is one that constructs for the viewer what we may refer to as 'vampire space'. The world of *Vampyr* is one situated ambiguously between life and death, a 'world of instability and shifting shadows where nothing is fixed or certain' (Wood 1974: 1), a world 'seen through a glass darkly' (Milne 1971: 108), a world in which 'people glide slowly through a vague, whitish mist like drowned men' (Neergaard 1950: 27). Like the vampire itself, space in *Vampyr* is 'fluid, plastic, uncertain' (Bordwell 1981: 98) creating a disorienting and nightmarish world where cause is severed from effect and in which the only temporal progression we can trust is 'the time that it takes for the film to be seen, the time it takes for the reels of the film to pass through the projector' (Grant 2003). This is a film in which the camera asserts itself as an 'independent factor' that 'need not be subservient to narrative causality' (Bordwell 1981: 105).

What *Vampyr* foregrounds above all else is *Vampyr*, the film *qua* film that challenges the conventions of Hollywood filmmaking. It is a film that emphasises the 'active role of the camera in constituting and questioning cinematic space' (ibid.) and one 'self-consciously created out of cinematic effects' (Grant 2003), leading Michael Grant to conclude that 'self-interrogation' is central to the film. There is a vampire in *Vampyr*, just as there is in *Dracula* – Marguerite Chopin, who provides the doctor with poison, vampirises Léone and, director-like, presumably orchestrates the behind-the-scenes actions and makes shadows dance. But it is the film *Vampyr*, not Marguerite Chopin, that occupies centre-stage, and in the same way that the protagonists in the typical vampire film must collect the clues, determine the cause of the affliction, decide upon a course of action and track and destroy the vampire, the viewer of *Vampyr* similarly must decide what is going on, collect the clues and try to make sense of a cinematic world that violates the conventions of representing reality encouraged by classical Hollywood cinema. *Vampyr* in this way 'undoes' *Dracula*, decentring – or defanging – the vampire by revealing that the true 'supernatural' potency lies with the camera. The vampire in *Vampyr* is a shadow, a death-in-life figure, but the true uncanniness of *Vampyr* is that it is no more or less supernatural than Allan Grey lying in his coffin, dreaming his own death.

The obvious point of reference for Dreyer's *Vampyr* is not Browning's *Dracula* of course, which was in production at the same time that Dreyer was filming, but Murnau's *Nosferatu*. Each film explores and experiments with the cinematic medium, associating the vampire – or the idea of vampirism – in the process with cinematic technology. But while Murnau's film expressionistically allows shadows to grow and stretch ominously, Dreyer's film severs their connection from any referent and gives them lives of their own. Detached from any corresponding person, they dig holes, shoot guns and dance. As such, they reveal the nature of cinema itself – detached shadows that dance across the screen cast only by the camera which has drained the life out of referents, preserving their essence in an uncanny state that is not life and is not death. The core of *Vampyr* is not the story of the vampire Marguerite Chopin, but of another vampire, the cinema itself.

Shadow Dancing: Shadow of the Vampire

The smartest, most explicit and most wonderful analysis of the vampire cinema, of the vampire as a cinematic creation and of the cinema as a type of vampire, is undoubtedly E. Elias Merhinge's *Shadow of the Vampire* – another film that shows the vampire cinema's metatextual preoccupations. That this is a film about the making of film and about the cinema itself is signalled right from the start since the film purports to be a sort of documentary-overview of the making of Murnau's *Nosferatu*. *Shadow of the Vampire* is a metafiction, a fictional narrative about the making of another fictional narrative and one that in the process raises interesting questions about the nature of the medium, in this case film, itself. The brilliant twist in *Shadow of the Vampire* is that Count Orlok, played by Willem Dafoe, is a real vampire masquerading as the human actor Max Schreck. As soon as we find ourselves caught up in the circle of contemplating a 'real' actor (Dafoe) playing a vampire (Count Orlok) playing a human (Max Schreck) playing a vampire (Count Orlok), we've already been interpolated into *Shadow of the Vampire*'s playful structure of meaning – its interrogation of the theatricality of the vampire genre and the cinema's role in producing the vampires it endlessly pursues and destroys.

Shadow of the Vampire begins precisely by foregrounding the cinema's manipulation of vision and framing of reality by opening with a reverse-shot through the camera of the director's eye (Murnau is played by John Malcovitch) as he prepares to begin shooting an early scene from *Nosferatu*. (Murnau, having lost his marbles, will insist at the end of the film that 'If it's not in frame, it doesn't exist!'). The film begins by focusing on the director and by raising issues of vision and perspective. The point of view then switches from the director's eye to what is seen through the camera. With interesting parallels to the scenes from Coppola's *Bram Stoker's Dracula* discussed above that masquerade as silent film footage, the iris of the camera opens and, shifting to black and white, we see *Nosferatu*'s Hutter (played here by Eddie Izzard) and Ellen (Catherine McCormack) enjoying a few moments of domestic bliss before Hutter's journey and its disastrous consequences. The point of view then shifts again to a God's eye shot that pulls back to reveal Hutter and Ellen as characters on a set. Colour returns – restoring 'reality' in contrast to the stagey-ness of the black and white scene – and, explicitly introducing the movie's theme of the cinema as vampire, Ellen announces her preference for performing in front of a live audience: 'A theatrical audience gives me life while this thing merely takes it from me.' Accentuating the foreshadowing introduced here, Murnau responds, 'Consider it a sacrifice for your art.' Both of these lines will take on special significance by the end of the film.

In contrast to Ellen's declaration that the camera drains her of life, Murnau emphasises the immortality that it offers in return. As the crew leaves the German sets behind and travels by train – the train cleverly christened 'Charon', an allusion to the Greek mythological ferryman who conveys the dead across the river Styx to Hades – Murnau in voiceover soliloquises, 'Our battle, our struggle is to create art. Our weapon is the moving picture. Because we have the moving picture, our paintings will grow and recede. Our poetry will be shadows that lengthen and conceal.

Our light will play across living faces that laugh and agonise. And our music will linger and finally overwhelm because it will have a context as certain as the grave.' This speech, which turns out to be an address to the cast and crew upon reaching their destination in Czechoslovakia, concludes with Murnau's assertion, 'We are scientists engaged in the creation of memory, but our memory will neither blur nor fade.'

Murnau's speech here is extraordinarily Derridean in its deconstruction of binary oppositions. Cinema is introduced as a sort of third term that interrupts the dichotomies of light and darkness, presence and absence, life and death. It captures the presence of death in life and preserves life after death. It drains the life out of Ellen only to reanimate her image again and again after her death in a ceaseless, traumatic repetition. It is living memory 'as certain as the grave', inscription that masquerades as speech, the shadow side of light itself – the cinema as vampire.

Not surprisingly given this connection that is established early on between cinema and death, Murnau, the director, throughout the film is paralleled with Count Orlok, the vampire. Murnau 'consumes' his actors – uses them as tools in the production of his art, drains them of life and vitality – just as readily as Orlok drinks their blood. This parallel is made explicit twice – both times by Count Orlok. Orlok first points out Murnau's lack of compassion and humanity when, having been chastised by Murnau for killing one of his crew, Orlok responds, 'Don't pretend you mourn, Herr Doktor. I know you.' Later, Orlok says to Murnau, 'You and I are not so different.' Both, the viewer realises, are monsters. Both are vampires masquerading as human. The parallel between them is cemented when their bargain is revealed: Count Orlok will play Max Schreck playing the vampire for Murnau's film in exchange for Ellen, and Murnau's film as a consequence will be a snuff film – the 'sacrifice for art' that Murnau mentions to Ellen at the start will be literalised, as will Ellen's concern about the draining effect of being filmed. She will be filmed being drained. She will be sacrificed for Murnau's art. She will die so that she can receive, in Murnau's words, 'ever-lasting life'.

The film culminates with an inspired effect that ensures that the parallel between cinema and vampire is unmistakable. As sunlight streams into the set that has been Ellen's death scene, Count Orlok and the film both go up in smoke. In *Nosferatu*, of course, the vampire grabs his chest, raises his arm upward and dissipates in a rather disappointing puff of smoke. In *Shadow*

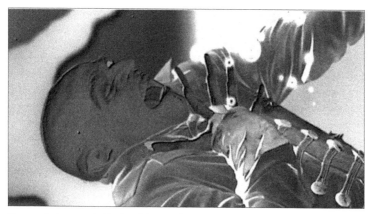

The vampire burns up in *Shadow of the Vampire*

of the Vampire, the light obliterates all as the film stock itself seems to melt and burn up. The vampire and the film are one – each survives by sucking the life out of others. Each is an uncanny creation of shadow and light that can only survive in the dark. Each is the uncanny projection of the other.

What *Nosferatu*, *Vampyr* and most especially *Shadow of the Vampire* make clear is not only that the cinematic vampire is a product of cinema's ability to manipulate representation through special effects and editing, but that this technological vampire is a stand-in for the uncanniness of the cinema itself. Like a vampire, the camera 'drains the life' out of the persons and objects represented, consigning them to an uncanny limbo zone between life and death – film creates legions of the undead that morph and transform before our eyes. Like a vampire, film shuns the light and only manifests in darkness. The vampire was present at the birth of cinema, watching in amazement at this hypnotic alter-ego, the shadow projection of itself.

Vampire Technology: Cronos

This chapter will end with some discussion of one of the strangest and most interesting entries into the category of vampire cinema: Guillermo del Toro's *Cronos*, which in a variety of ways brings together several of the treads introduced in the course of this chapter. It is a story of infection, addiction and parasitism. The movie begins by quickly establishing its fantastic premise: in a prologue, the viewer is flatly informed that in the year 1537, an alchemist fleeing the Spanish Inquisition arrived in Mexico where he 'invented the key to eternal life', his 'Cronos device'. In 1937, four hundred years later, he died when a building collapsed, leaving a corpse with pure white, leathery skin. The viewer is told that the police, investigating his villa, never revealed what they found, but the viewer is shown glimpses of a naked human body suspended upside down and bowls filled with a red substance.

Flashing forward to the present, the movie proper begins with the introduction of Jésus Gris (played by Argentine actor Federico Luppi), the elderly proprietor of an antique store, and his granddaughter Aurora (Tamara Shanath). After some strange incidents surrounding a statue of an angel occur (a stranger pays special attention to it, roaches crawl out of it), Gris investigates and discovers an ornate, golden, scarab-like device in the base that exudes spidery legs that grip him tightly and a scorpion-like stinger that pierces his skin and injects him with something. Soon after, Gris finds himself growing younger and more energetic – as well as addicted to the device's injections. He also, however, develops a thirst for blood. What the viewer learns is that this is the Cronos device. Inside a mesh of gears and cogs and wheels is an insect that provides eternal youth and life in exchange for blood.

Unfortunately for Gris, he has accidentally stumbled upon the device for which rich capitalist Dieter de la Guardia (Claudio Brook) has been searching for years. De la Guardia, who is dying of an unspecified illness, dispatches his sadistic, egotistical cousin Angel de la Guardia (Ron Perlman, in his first collaboration with del Toro) to retrieve the device. When Gris refuses to hand it over, Angel beats him up and pushes him over a cliff in a car. Gris, however, is now immortal – or undead – and, although trapped in the car and exhibiting no signs of life, is not dead. The world, however, thinks he is – a funeral is held for him (in perhaps the movie's most gruesome moment, a mortician prepares him for the funeral by sewing his mouth shut) and he narrowly escapes cremation by escaping from his coffin while no one is watching.

Gris is now a repulsive, zombie-like figure with rotting flesh. He cannot go to his wife, but reveals himself to his granddaughter, who shelters him in her attic playhouse. Since sunlight now burns him, he sleeps during the day in a large chest. In order to find out what has happened to him and if there is a cure, he and Aurora break into Dieter de la Guardia's chamber, looking for a book that constitutes an instruction manual for the Cronos device. After explaining to Gris that he can peel off his decaying skin to reveal a new, pure white layer beneath, de la Guardia tries to 'cure' Gris by stabbing him through the heart (the only way to kill him). Gris is saved when his granddaughter brains de la Guardia with one of his own canes and then Gris ghoulishly drinks from the freely flowing blood.

De la Guardia's cousin, Angel, now arrives on the scene and pursues Gris and Aurora onto the roof of the complex. Gris, who realises he cannot be killed, tackles Angel and the two plummet from the roof through the glass ceiling of a building below. Aurora makes her way down and Gris, who arises from the rubble with shards of glass protruding from his body, must exert all his willpower not to drink Aurora's blood. It is this battle to contain his thirst that convinces him that the Cronos device must be destroyed and he crushes it. The odd final tableau of the film shows the snow-white Gris in bed, presumably dying, with his wife and granddaughter by his side.

Cronos is innovative in a number of ways. To begin with, as is the case with *Interview With the Vampire*, released one year after *Cronos*, it shifts the conventional point of view away from that of the vampire hunter to that of the vampire himself as he attempts to understand and grapple with what has happened to him. The sympathetic protagonist of *Cronos* is Gris, who unwittingly activates the Cronos device thereby setting into motion the sequence of events leading to his transformation and ultimate death. In *Cronos*, however, unlike in *Interview With the Vampire*, there are vampire hunters – but the conventional good/evil polarity has been reversed. Angel and Dieter de la Guardia, who seek to recover the Cronos device at all costs, are no Crew of Light but rather villains who are in essence the film's true vampires. In contrast to Gris, who is a doting grandfather, loving husband to his wife, Mercedes, and small business owner, Dieter, the arch-capitalist, seems to detest his cousin, and Angel not only rejoices when he discovers his uncle bleeding on the floor, but finishes him off with a foot on his neck. (This parallel between de la Guardia and a vampire is accentuated by the fact that both de la Guardia and the blood-drinking insect at the heart of the Cronos device survive by remaining within hermetically-sealed chambers.)

Beyond this, *Cronos* takes all the elements of the conventional vampire story – an 'undead' character with a thirst for blood who hides from daylight and can only be killed by a stake through the heart – and introduces an especially intriguing twist: vampirism is here technologically mediated, the product of a mechanical apparatus, the Cronos device, that when placed over the heart drinks blood and provides eternal life – and a thirst for blood – in exchange. Gris, in Ann Davies' estimation (2008), is thus literally a sort of cyborg, kept alive by a machine that itself is an odd synthesis of natural and mechanical – an insect hermetically sealed within a technological carapace resembling a combination of spider, scarab and scorpion. What *Cronos* shows us is that vampires are always cyborgs, always produced and defined by the technologies needed to detect, identify and destroy them. They are situated and defined in relation to scientific discourses of identification and categorisation. They are produced by cinematic special effects. And they are ultimately creatures of shadow and light, projected onto the screen by technological devices crafted for this purpose. To view the vampire cinema then is to engage with desires and anxieties concerning the human relationship with technology.

3   VAMPIRE OTHERNESS

In the Hammer Studios classic from 1958, *The Horror of Dracula* – the film that introduced the world to Christopher Lee in the role of the world's most famous vampire – the Crew of Light scours the town (apparently somewhere in Germany) for Dracula's coffin. Lucy Holmwood (Carol Marsh) is dead twice over having been bitten and then staked and the viewer knows that Mina (Melissa Stribbing) has already been nibbled on by the master vampire. Van Helsing (Peter Cushing) and Arthur Holmwood (Michael Gough) trace the intended destination of Dracula's coffin to a funeral home operated curiously by one 'J. Marx', but the coffin is not there. Returning to Arthur's home, they keep watch all night but, despite their vigilance, somehow Dracula still manages to penetrate their defenses and get to Mina again – and this is because he is not outside at all, but already in the house hiding in the cellar. Imported from central Europe into Germany by J. Marx (one listing above K. Marx in the phone book), the vampire lurks in the basement of a respectable home, draining the populace and converting them into vampires that prey upon others. And in this film that pioneered Technicolor for the vampire genre, the vampire is literally 'a red' as vividly red blood splashes his coffin in the opening credits and later runs down his face.

Condensed in this way, it is hard not to read *The Horror of Dracula* as a manifestation of the 1950s 'Red Scare', the rampant and at times rabid hysteria concerning the spread of communism into Western democracies. In this film, the (literally) unholy force from central Europe comes to Germany by way of Marx and converts 'normal' everyday people into monsters who then turn upon those they love. In keeping with a similar Red Scare film released two years earlier, *The Invasion of the Body Snatchers* (1956), what is particularly disconcerting about vampirism is that vampires, such as the vampirised Lucy and Mina, are indistinguishable from 'normal' human beings. From Bolsheviks in the washroom to reds in the basement, *The Horror of Dracula* and other 1950s films that play on Red Scare anxiety suggest the vampire-communist infection is upon us and upstanding supporters of democracy must remain vigilant against the predations of those who would suck out our life force and transform us into mindless clones.

The irony of figuring communism as a form of vampirism is that the vampire is precisely the metaphor used by Karl Marx to figure fat-cat *capitalists*. In a famous passage from *Capital*, Marx writes, 'Capital is dead labour which, vampire-like, lives only by sucking labour, and lives the more, the more labour it sucks' (1976: 342). As explicated by Rob Latham, for Marx 'the capitalist-factory system is a regime of avid vampirism whose victims are transformed into undead extensions of its own vast, insensate, endlessly feeding body' (2002: 3). In other words, capitalists are vampires who live off the life force of their employees.

That the same metaphor can turn both ways, can be used to figure both a thing and its opposite, communism and capitalism, is indicative of both the extraordinary flexibility and potency of the idea of vampirism. Alan S. Ambrico and Lance Svehla capture this sense of vampiric plasticity in their analysis of Wes Craven's *Dracula 2000* when they assert that, 'Whether represented as demonised monopolist, stereotyped Jew, feudal aristocrat, or iconoclastic youth, what remains in all manifestations of the vampire is its ability to become what the culture both desires and reviles, to seduce in the act of producing fear' (2006: 21). Milly Williamson similarly notes the flexibility of the vampire metaphor in the introduction to her book *The Lure of the Vampire* when she observes that critics have variously explicated the vampire as figuring 'a voraciously sexual woman, a hyper-sexual African, a hypnotic Jewish invader, an effeminate or homosexual man' (2005: 1). What Ambrico, Svehla and Williamson thus remark upon is that the vampire functions as a convenient catch-all figuration for social otherness – an analysis that echoes author Anne Rice's comment that the vampire is a 'metaphor for the outsider' (see Martin 1991: 38). The threatening other – whether sexually, racially, religiously, economically or ideologically – invariably is figured as a type of vampire that generally seduces, often converts, and always drains us. The cinematic vampire thus emerges as the overdetermined condensation of a constellation of cultural anxieties and desires.

As discussed in the preceding chapters, celluloid vampire narratives always engage to greater or lesser extents with ideologies of gender and technology. This chapter will switch the emphasis to race, which in my opinion is the issue at the centre of much contemporary vampire cinema. After looking at the way the always implicit issue of race in relation to the vampire became suddenly visible in the 1970s blaxploitation films *Blacula* and *Scream Blacula Scream* (1973), as well as in the artier *Ganja & Hess* (1973), I will consider the ways in which the *Blade* and *Underworld* series articulate similar philosophies of race with miscegenation as central to each. The discussion of race in *Underworld* will lead into a discussion of class since the two topics are inextricably interconnected and this will allow me to bring Marx back into the discussion while considering *Blood for Dracula* (also known as *Andy Warhol's Dracula* (1973)) and George A. Romero's *Martin* (1977). Finally, this chapter will conclude with some consideration of a very interesting recent vampire movie that seems to have flown under the radar, *The Breed* (2001), which in fascinating ways mixes race and class with religion and makes clear the overdetermined origins of the vampire – the ways in which it always condenses multiple anxieties and desires into one supersaturated (and often quite sexy) body.

Race and the Vampire

In Stephen Arata's important analysis of Bram Stoker's *Dracula*, he makes a very convincing case for Stoker's vampire as embodying anxieties about race and what he terms 'reverse colonization' (1997: 465). Arata proposes that Dracula's invasion of England reflects and plays on Victorian England's fears of racial enervation and declining world status. The novel dramatises a nightmare of reverse colonisation in which racially inferior others, embodied by Stoker's Transylvanian Count, invade the heart of the British empire, endangering 'Britain's integrity as a nation at the same time that [they imperil] the personal integrity of individual citizens' (ibid.). Arata concludes that 'through the vampire myth, Stoker gothicises the political threats to Britain caused by the [perceived] enervation of the Anglo-Saxon "race"' (1997: 466).

Arata's argument concerning the racial anxieties underlying Stoker's vampire novel clearly also applies to much early vampire cinema. In almost all pre-Hammer Studios films, particularly those based on Stoker's *Dracula*, the vampire is an exotic invader who comes from the East. In *Nosferatu*, the grotesque vampire comes from Transylvania – as does the much more suave and sophisticated vampire Dracula played by Bela Lugosi in the 1931 Tod Browning production and Countess Zaleska (Gloria Holden) in *Dracula's Daughter* (1936). In *Son of Dracula* (1943), the mysterious Count Alucard (Lon Cheney Jr) travels from Hungary to the American Deep South and, as near as one can tell, the vampire Marguerite Chopin (Henriette Gerard) in Dreyer's *Vampyr* also comes from Hungary. In all of these early vampire films, the vampire is an invader, a mysterious other who comes from elsewhere to prey upon the populace, while the film in turn plays upon all the racist and xenophobic fears of the audience.

Vampire films, starting in the late 1950s, follow two basic trajectories: either the vampire arrives from elsewhere (which is the case for nearly all vampire films that draw their inspiration either from Stoker's *Dracula* or Sheridan Le Fanu's 'Carmilla' (1872)) or the protagonist arrives at a location under the sway of a vampire's controlling gaze. (A variant on this – usually in sequels – is the revivification of the vampire who is already there, having previously come from elsewhere). So, for example, in Hammer Studios' 'Carmilla' adaptation, *The Vampire Lovers* (1970), Carmilla (Ingrid Pitt) arrives mysteriously at Emma Morton's residence. Vampires arrive from out of town in films including the Japanese film *Lake of Dracula* (1971), the TV mini-series adaptation of Stephen King's *'Salem's Lot* (with James Mason as the Nosferatu-esque vampire Straker), *Fright Night*, *Nadja*, *Habit*, *Dracula 2000*, *30 Days of Night* and *Let the Right One In*. In vampire science fiction films including *Planet of Blood* (memorable only for featuring a very young Dennis Hopper), *Lifeforce* (1985) and *Vampirella* (1996), the vampires actually come from outer space. In contrast, it is the protagonist who encroaches on the vampire's territory in films including the Mexican 'Dracula on the hacienda' film *El Vampiro*, the Italian *Black Sunday* (1960, directed by Mario Bava and featuring Barbara Steele as the vampire-witch Asa Vadja), the Roman Polanski-directed *The Fearless Vampire Killers* (1967), Hammer Studios' *Captain Kronos – Vampire Hunter* (1974), Robert Rodrigeuz's *From Dusk Till Dawn*, *The Lost Boys*, *John Carpenter's Vampires*, and the film adaptation of *Twilight*.

Mobility and crossing of not only geographical but social and psychic borders is central to the vampire narrative. Either the vampire arrives from elsewhere to interrupt the day-to-day existence of his or her new locale or the protagonist arrives at a place marked by some fundamental social difference – the superstitiousness of backwater villagers, the lawlessness of Mexico or Santa Carla, California, etc. But more fundamental than the question of where the vampire comes from is the simple question of 'what is it?' Is the vampire human or something else? And it is with this question of definition that issues of race are introduced most explicitly.

Blaxploitation and the Vampire: Blacula and Scream Blacula Scream

'Blaxploitation' films of the 1970s targeted urban black audiences by utilising black casts and subject matter intended to interest persons of African descent. Given the flexibility of the vampire as metaphor, as well as the established celluloid vampire tradition, blaxploitation vampire films seem a given and, indeed, two blaxploitation films (and possibly three, if one includes *Ganja & Hess* – more on this below) took on the vampire genre and in provocative ways 'blacken' the vampire – that is, they reveal the racialised roots of the vampire mythos. *Blacula* and *Scream Blacula Scream* both centre on the vampire Mamuwalde (William H. Marshall), christened 'Blacula' by none other than Dracula (Charles Macaulay) himself. In each film, the black vampire literally is two-faced as he alternates between being cultured, suave and sophisticated and animalistic, destructive and vengeful. In each film, Blacula also struggles with the social alienation that results from his 'curse'. None of this is new to the vampire genre; what is new, however, is that the vampire's rage and social alienation are explicitly connected to racism and the legacy of the slave trade. What both *Blacula* and *Scream Blacula Scream* ultimately illustrate are the damaging effects of racist ideologies that connect difference with monstrosity and thus, through a form of self-fulfilling prophecy, give birth to nightmares.

That white racism transforms black men into monsters is in fact illustrated in the opening moments of *Blacula*. In the prologue to the film, the viewer is introduced to Prince Mamuwalde, a cultured, handsome and dignified African ruler in Western dress, and his wife Luva (Vonetta McGee) who have travelled to Transylvania in the year 1780 to seek the help of Count Dracula in suppressing the slave trade. Dracula, it turns out, is a racist with no qualms whatsoever concerning black slavery. After he leers lecherously at Luva, Mamuwalde indignantly characterises him as 'behaving like some animal', prompting Dracula's racist retort that he is no one to talk because Africans in general are only slightly removed from animals. A fight breaks out, Dracula looses his hideous vampire brides on the couple and then, once Mamuwalde and Luva have been subdued, Dracula himself vampirises Mamuwalde, christens him 'Blacula', condemns him to join the ranks of the undead, and seals him in a coffin. Luva is sealed in a room with Mamuwalde and left to starve to death.

Flash forward almost two centuries later. An interracial – and extremely stereotyped – gay couple purchases castle Dracula and all its furnishings, including the coffin housing Blacula that is discovered in a secret room, and imports them to the US. Predictably, the coffin is opened and Blacula is set loose upon modern-day Los Angeles. The film's twist is that Mamuwalde encounters Tina (also played by Vonetta McGee) whom he believes to be his reincarnated bride, Luva. His courtship of Tina brings him to the attention of Dr Gordon Thomas (Thalmus Rasulala), who is helping the police investigate the strange murders occurring in LA and who conveniently is dating Tina's sister, Michelle (Denise Nicholas). Thomas slowly reaches the conclusion that Mamuwalde is the vampire and, after convincing the white police commissioner Lt Jack Peters (Gordon Pinsent) that a vampire is on the prowl in Los Angeles, the film culminates in a confrontation between the police and Mamuwalde in which Tina is shot. Mamuwalde turns her into a vampire to save her life, but she is then staked. Distraught by losing his love twice, Blacula walks into the sun, which kills him.

Blacula obviously is organised around the 'gimmick' of a black vampire. What it makes clear from its opening moments, however, is that the vampire genre both in literature and in cinema has been organised around the racialised 'othering' of the vampire. The source of vampirism in the popular imagination is always elsewhere – central Europe in Stoker, Styria in LeFanu, Egypt in Anne Rice, etc., and the vampire thus is derived from different racial stock and is defined by different blood. Simultaneously debased aristocrat with enervated blood and animalistic subaltern, the vampire not only invades from elsewhere but presents the potent threat of contamination of blood.

The confrontation between Dracula and Mamuwalde in the prologue to *Blacula* consciously inverts the racist assumption of white superiority by making clear that Dracula, the white European aristocrat, is the animal. It is Dracula who, in response to Mamuwalde's characterisation of the slave trade as barbarism, states while ogling Luva that he 'finds some merit in barbarity' and who literally and figuratively is motivated by his blood-lust to prey upon and enslave Mamuwalde. As Leerom Medovoi puts it, Mamuwalde is 'subjugated by a white sadist, re-named after his master, torn away from his beloved, and literally forced to make the middle passage in a coffin' (1998: 7). The idea of vampirism as a type of addiction and the vampire as a 'slave' to his thirst is a relatively common theme in vampire cinema; *Blacula* interestingly literalises this metaphor by linking vampirism explicitly to the eighteenth-century slave trade. The result is that the refined Mamuwalde, the 'crystallisation' of African culture according to Luva, is transformed into a monster. He is made into a vampire by an existing vampire – Dracula – who himself is shown to be an avatar of racist vampiric ideology, a social system that sanctions brutality and exploitation predicated upon pseudo-scientific ideas concerning blood and race. What *Blacula* ultimately demonstrates is that vampirism – despite always being projected as coming from afar – inevitably begins at home.

What *Blacula* thus chronicles is the transformation of a prince into a monster as a result of racist exploitation. White culture gives birth to the monsters it fears. What is particularly interesting is that throughout both *Blacula* and *Scream Blacula Scream*, as noted, Mamuwalde/Blacula is literally a two-faced Jeckle and Hyde figure. When attending social functions, interacting with the other characters, and courting Tina, he appears stately and refined. When he transforms into Blacula, however, his face is covered in hair and he becomes a creature of pure rage – he literally becomes the animal that Dracula assumes him to be because of his African origins in the prologue to the film. But his animalistic rage is not presented as some atavistic race memory embedded in the genes, but rather as the result of the curse of Dracula, the predations of barbaric white culture. The vampire's rage is here, as Medovoi appreciates, 'born of the slave trade' (1998: 8).

If *Blacula* shows the way in which the insistent correlation between racial difference and monstrosity creates monsters, *Scream Blacula Scream* shows the ramifications of this among the American black community and, in keeping with the Black Pride movement of the 1970s (one working title for the film was *Blacula is Beautiful*), seeks ways to undo the damage and – quite literally in this film – to exorcise the haunting demon of slavery. The movie begins with a scene of the transferral of power within an American

Blacula: The civilised side...

... and the animal

voodoo cult. The dying voodoo priestess, Mama Loa (Anita Bell), selects her adopted apprentice, Lisa Fortier (Pam Grier), as her successor – much to the dismay and outrage of cult member Willis (Richard Lawson). In order to seek revenge, Willis buys the bones of Blacula from a former voodoo shaman (Bernie Hamilton) and performs a voodoo ritual to revivify the vampire. His ritual is a success but he finds that he cannot control Blacula or order him to do his bidding. Instead, he is enslaved by Blacula.

What is particularly interesting about the voodoo ritual and revivification sequence is that it takes place within a large – almost plantation house-like – mansion for which Willis is serving as caretaker while the (presumably white) owners are away. Willis is thus engaged in a very complicated racial negotiation; while masquerading to a certain extent as the rich owner of the mansion, he seeks to enslave his former friends and cult members by performing a voodoo ritual and summoning a black vampire. His intent to enslave, however, backfires as he finds himself enslaved by the black vampire he would direct against other blacks – a vampire who then appropriates the mansion as his lair and, working from the heart of white capitalism, ventures forth into the world. Blacula here, dispossessing the sham black owner, has in a sense made Dracula's castle his own and develops over the course of the film an assemblage of slaves, both white and black, who must respect his commands and do his bidding.

As in *Blacula*, however, the vampire in *Scream Blacula Scream* performs two identities. He is not just the hairy-faced monster who enslaves those upon whom he preys, he is also again Mamuwalde, the stately, refined and well-groomed gentleman who can discourse knowledgeably about African artefacts and culture at parties and night clubs, and his objective within the film is to exorcise the beast part – the literal legacy of his enslavement by Dracula – and to live purely as a civilised human being. When he meets Lisa Fortier at a party, he sees in her voodoo powers the opportunity to lift his vampiric curse and engages her to perform an exorcism for which she prepares a voodoo doll version of him. The ritual appears to be working, but is interrupted and, in the conclusion of the film, Blacula is dispatched when Lisa stakes the voodoo doll.

But the true object of the film's ire is not Blacula, who cannot control his actions, but instead African Americans who choose to exploit other African Americans and who ape white culture. In perhaps the film's most telling scene, Mamuwalde, having left the party at which he first meets Lisa, is solicited by a black prostitute and then confronted by two black pimps who insult him for having rejected her advances and attempt to mug him. As Blacula easily fends off and dispatches his assailants, he berates them, telling them, 'You've made a slave of your sister and you're still slaves, imitating your masters'. This characterisation also applies to the unsympathetic character Willis, who lives in a large mansion that isn't his and who would use Blacula to terrorise his former friends. In contrast, the heroes of the film are Justin (Don Mitchell) an ex-police officer turned philanthropist with an impressive collection of African antiquities and Lisa, a voodoo priestess. The message of the film thus is that the path toward overcoming the debilitating legacy of slavery for African Americans lies in social solidarity and embracing, not denying, one's ethnic heritage. What Blacula enacts by enslaving Willis and the others upon whom he preys is the conflicted identity of the outsider within 1970s white American culture and it is because he cannot free himself of the haunting legacy of slavery that he must be destroyed at the end of the film – significantly by a strong, black woman who accepts and utilises African religious practice. Both *Blacula* and *Scream Blacula Scream* thus suggest that, although white hegemony has the potential to turn black men into monsters, rage and self-hatred can be overcome through a process of standing together and living authentically.

A Blood Society – Ganja & Hess

Ganja & Hess apparently was not what it was supposed to be. As Manthia Diawara and Phyllis R. Klotman tell it, the film was commissioned to be a blaxploitation film in keeping with the ethos established by other films of the early 1970s such as *Shaft* (1971) and *Blacula* – a 'black version of white vampire films' that would appeal to urban black audiences (1991: 299). The film, however, was withdrawn from general release when, despite receiving the Critics' Choice prize at the Cannes Film Festival and many favourable reviews, the producers discovered that writer and director Bill Gunn had created a complicated, slow-moving and atmospheric vampire film very far from their original expectations.

As Diawara and Klotman note, *Ganja & Hess* is difficult to summarise because the film violates conventional linear plot development and easy categorisation of characters. Schematically, however, the film progresses as follows: a brief introduction explains that Dr Hess Green (played by Duane Jones of *Night of the Living Dead* fame), who holds PhDs in both anthropology and geology and is currently studying the 'ancient black culture of Myrthia', was stabbed ritualistically with a 'diseased' Myrthinian dagger causing him to become 'addicted' (to what is not specified at this point) and making him immortal. Dr Green, the viewer subsequently learns is a handsome, cultured aesthete with a Rolls Royce; a mansion filled with African, Asian and Western art objects; a butler; and a driver. The culture he is studying, Myrthia, is an extinct African tribe of the Niger Delta that practiced ritualistic blood drinking which, the viewer is told through song, produced a race of vampires.

Complications ensue when Dr Green takes on an assistant, George Meda (played by the film's director Bill Gunn), who is subject to depression and incidences of psychotic behaviour. After contemplating suicide one evening – in an eerie scene with overtones of lynching, Meda (who, like Green, is a black man) has strung a noose up on a tree and is talked down by Hess who mainly seems concerned about what his white neighbours will think – Meda has a psychotic break and attacks Green in his sleep, stabbing him three times with the Myrthinian dagger. Meda then bathes, seemingly baptising himself, and proceeds to shoot himself through the heart. Dr Green magically is unharmed, but finds himself governed by an unquenchable thirst for blood and haunted by visions of the Queen of Myrthia (Mabel King), who beckons to him in dreams and visions. In order to avoid controversy, Green stores Meda's body in a large walk-in freezer in his basement. To satisfy his thirst for blood, he robs blood banks and preys upon prostitutes.

Some time after Meda's suicide, his attractive and assertive wife, Ganja (Marlene Clark), comes calling, looking for her husband. She and Green quickly end up in bed together and the relationship continues despite her discovery of Meda's body in Green's freezer. The two are married and Green, unwilling to lose her, initiates her into the blood cult by stabbing her ritualistically with the African dagger and he then ignites her thirst for blood by bringing home a handsome young man (played by Richard Harrow) who, literally, becomes dinner. The movie culminates with Green destroying himself by allowing the shadow of the cross to fall upon his heart while Ganja continues on, seemingly welcoming a new vampire lover, the young man from dinner, into the luxurious mansion that is now hers.

In Diawara and Klotman's appraisal, *Ganja & Hess* is ultimately about Ganja, a 'contemporary black woman [who] is tired of being subservient to the church and to black men' (1991: 314). They continue: 'She's glad that Meda and Hess, the self-destructive artist and the bourgeois patriarch, are gone. It is in this sense that we understand her cunning smile at the end. She's in command' (ibid.). While I do not disagree with this consideration of the film's feminist subtext, an over-emphasis on Ganja at the film's conclusion not only plays down the extent to which she is in command from the moment she enters the film (in her first meeting with Green, she assumes that he is a servant rather than the owner of the mansion and instructs him to let his boss know she is there), but also neglects the extent to which the film uses the theme of vampirism explicitly to address the negotiation of race and class in 1970s America.

The employment of the motif of vampirism as social commentary is made apparent when considering the two suicides that organise the formal structure of the movie. Early in the film, Meda, having abandoned his plan to hang himself, explains to Green that during a previous schizophrenic episode, he became aware of the strange sensation of being divided into two – into a victim and a murderer. He held a knife to his own throat, but couldn't go through with the act. Later, believing that he has murdered Dr Green after stabbing him with the Myrthinian dagger, he types a diffuse, poetic suicide letter, addressing it 'To the black male children'. The letter begins by explaining that 'philosophy is a prison; it disregards the uncustomary things about you'. Then, after characterising black male children as the 'despised of the earth', the letter concludes with the assertion that love is all there is and that black male youth 'are cannon fodder in its defense'. Meda, it turns out, is – as per his schizoid fantasy – both victim and murderer. His suicide note makes clear that he feels himself to be a victim of a racist society that reviles black men. While at the end of his letter he counsels love, it is clear that he has rage in his heart and that he loathes both himself and the world around him.

Diawara and Klotman read Meda's attack on Dr Green as an Oedipal scenario in which Meda is attempting to kill a father figure in order to secure his own identity. While there certainly may be an element of this involved, Meda's sense of being both victim and murderer when combined with his letter addressed to black male youth which tells them that there is no place for them in white Western philosophy seems more clearly intended to reflect the alienation experienced by black men in 1970s America. His killing of Dr Green express his rage at a black man who apes white culture – who lives in a mansion in an all-white neighbourhood, who is fluent in French and sends his son to boarding school, who employs black servants, and who collaborates with the socio-economic system that disenfranchises black men like Meda.

Meda's rage turns Dr Green into a literal vampire. The film suggests, however, that for Dr Green to feed upon Meda would be redundant because

Meda all along has been, to shift his metaphor, vampire fodder; he has metaphorically been preyed upon, sucked dry, and turned into a monster by the same racist social structure illustrated in Richard Wright's *Native Son* (1940) that forces black men to become schizophrenic – to live a form of 'double consciousness' as articulated by W. E. B. Du Bois in which black men are always aware of themselves as black, as not white, as outside the structures of power that organise American society. Meda, who when he first arrives at Dr Green's mansion hasn't had a good meal in days, is both literally and figuratively starving, denied as he is the status and self-affirmation he craves. Symbolically emasculated by the weight of cultural expectations that position him as a servant and as inferior, as well as by a wife, Ganja, who is far more assertive than he is and appears not to care for him very much, he vacillates between self-hatred and explosive rage. Invited inside Dr Green's mansion, he attacks his host and then, repulsed at the monster he has become, commits suicide. But what the film suggests is that Meda was the living dead before he ever arrived at Dr Green's mansion, both animated and murdered by a racist culture.

Meda's suicide, however, is not the film's only suicide. Indeed, in the same way that Meda shoots himself through the heart with a cross promi-nently displayed in the background, Dr Green, after having gone to church and been blessed, commits suicide by allowing the shadow of the cross to fall upon his heart. This structural repetition of the suicides of the film's two primary male protagonists makes clear that, despite Green's wealth and refinement, he and Meda are mirror reflections of one another. Like Meda, Green too is both a victim and a murderer. Before he is even stabbed by Meda and transformed into a vampire, Green interestingly has his own schizophrenic dreams in which a vision of a masked, laughing white man in a tuxedo (apparently one of the rich benefactors or board members of the museum associated with his research) competes with a vision of the Queen of Myrthia in calling to him. He is divided between his participation in the white man's world of power and affluence and his African roots.

According to Diawara and Klotman, *Ganja & Hess* 'indicts Hess Green's very wealth and class position as vampirism' (1991: 301). But while Green is clearly a 'pleasure-loving materialist' (1991: 302), the film appears less critical of his wealth *per se* than of his 'Uncle Tom-ism' and willingness to exploit others to satisfy his needs and desires. As mentioned earlier, when Meda is in the tree threatening to hang himself, Green mainly appears concerned about what his white neighbours will think and demonstrates no real concern or sympathy for Meda. In response to Meda's explanation that he suffers from depression and that his suicide attempt has nothing to do with Green, he responds that since it is his tree and his rope, he is unavoidably implicated, which would then give the authorities license to come snooping around his property.

The callousness of Green's character is developed even more explicitly in the two scenes in which he drives into the city to feed on prostitutes. The first scene gives the viewer latitude to excuse Green's preying upon other African Americans. The prostitute (Candece Tarpley) is shown to be in league with her pimp (Tommy Lane) to rob and possibly to murder Green. When the pimp breaks into the prostitute's room during the sexual encounter while the prostitute screams 'kill him', the viewer has little sympathy for either. The second scene of Green's predations, however, is quite different. This time, Green is shown going into an urban townhouse with a woman with a baby. While the encounter is not shown, the aftermath is: the woman lies bloody and dead upon her bed while a baby cries in the background. The slow rocking of the camera communicates the sense of psychological distress – of the world being off-kilter.

Nowhere, however, is Green's selfishness and willingness to exploit others for personal gain more clearly marked by the film than in the dinner party sequence. Green has already turned Ganja into a vampire without her permission or desire because he is unwilling to lose her. In order to ignite her thirst, he brings home a handsome young black man (Harrow) who volunteers at an urban recreation centre – he is someone who helps others rather than feeds off of them. A fantasised sexual encounter between Ganja and the young man appears to become real as we see the two engage in the film's most explicit representation of sexual intimacy and then the scene transforms into one of vampirism as Ganja feeds on the young man. Later, the two deposit the plastic-shrouded corpse in a field, despite Ganja's panicked assertion that she can still see him breathing. Having left a baby motherless – and possibly to die – Dr Green here has again robbed the black community of its future in the form of a handsome and promising young man marked by his social altruism.

As with Meda, Green appears to choose suicide because he can no longer reconcile his schizoid existence as both black and white, victim and murderer. Torn by his desire for wealth and material pleasures – and subsequently by his literal thirst for blood – he first must pass as white and then simply as human. But his continued status and ultimately his survival depend upon his exploitation of others and he finally chooses to die – literally and figuratively in the shadow of the cross – rather than to continue as a vampire, as someone forced to pass for something he is not and as someone who survives by draining away the life force of others

There is not space here to give *Ganja & Hess* the complete analysis it deserves – a more nuanced consideration of the film would need to attend carefully to the role Christianity plays within the film as a countervailing force both to contemporary capitalist exploitation and to the African Mrythinian blood cult (both Meda and George seek spiritual redemption), as well as to the implications of Ganja's seeming embrace of her vampiric existence at the end. For our purposes here, what I wish to highlight is the 1970s 'blackening' of the vampire. What *Blacula*, *Scream Blacula Scream* and *Ganja & Hess* reveal through the 'gimmick' of the black vampire is that the vampire has always been racialised as an 'ethnic' outsider 'passing' as human. Originating in central Europe or Africa or South America, the vampire is a creature marked by different, contaminating blood and the threat – or, as we shall see, promise – it represents is always that of racial mixture.

Contamination as the Key: Answering the Race Question in Blade and Underworld

The *Blacula* films and *Ganja & Hess* make explicit the racialisation of the vampire. In keeping with 1970s events and racial consciousness movements, these films engage in a very explicit discourse about race, demonstrating the ways in which capitalist exploitation and an oppressive racial hierarchy conspire to drain black men of hope and vitality and transform them into monsters that turn upon others and themselves. *Scream Blacula Scream* and *Ganja & Hess* in particular hold up for harsh critique black men who white-identify and participate in the exploitation of African Americans and suggest solidarity of religious practice (in *Scream Blacula Scream* Afro-centric voodoo; in *Ganja & Hess* fundamentalist Christianity) as recuperative strategies to address the disenfranchisement and emasculation of American black men. What happens between the 1970s and the 1990s is that the issue of race in the vampire film – having had its moment in the sun, so to speak – sinks back beneath the surface. In a terrifically provocative way, however, race becomes the organising problematic – the unspoken nexus of affect – in modern vampire films and most especially in the very popular *Blade* and *Underworld* franchises. I will argue that both these series talk constantly about race in Western culture without ever stating this explicitly and, more provocatively still, both series propose the same answer to the 'racial question': miscegenation. Shifting away from paranoia about the contamination of blood, the modern vampire film instead suggests that the solution to racism and racial violence in modern Western culture is precisely the mixing of bloodlines. Those who remain wed to the 'purity' of bloodlines in the modern vampire film are shown to be racists, often with genocidal intentions, wed to old and discredited ideas. Contamination of blood is the solution, not the problem.

The Blade Series

The *Blade* films, as discussed briefly in the last chapter, are insistently organised around issues of race. At the centre of the films, which are loosely based around the Marvel Comics character of the same name, is the black vampire, Blade (Wesley Snipes) who has special abilities because he was born soon after his mother was bitten by a vampire. As a result, he is a 'daywalker', a human/vampire hybrid whose powers outstrip those of both races. He possesses all the preternatural strength, agility, speed and recuperative abilities of the vampire, while also being able to move about during daylight. As a 'hybrid', he also possesses the moral compass and empathy for 'mortals' that the vampires in the series, believing themselves to be superior to humans (a belief held even by those vampires who were 'turned', that is, who were once human) lack. His unique blood is revealed to be the key to antagonist vampire Deacon Frost's (Stephen Dorff) plan to enslave humanity in eponymous first *Blade* film from 1998.

What the first *Blade* film details is that a racial hierarchy exists even within the vampire world, with those who were born vampires considering themselves more racially pure than those who were 'turned'. Frost, a turned vampire, encounters resistance and discrimination from the old guard, the pure blood vampire elders (including, in a lovely bit of intertextual casting, one played by Udo Kier whose vampire movie pedigree is lengthy), who reject his proposal that vampires should assert their superiority by

Blade prepares to battle vampires

enslaving all humans – whom Frost regards as inferior beasts of burden and a source of food. The elders ultimately are swept out of the way as Frost pushes his programme forward and it is up to Blade – with the assistance of an 'anticoagulant' developed by sexy haematologist Dr Karen Jensen (N'Bushe Wright) – to vanquish Frost when he becomes inhabiting by La Magra, the vampire 'blood god'.

Blade is a thinly-veiled allegory of American race relations in which vampires stand in for whites, and humans in general for racial minorities. The (white) vampires, defined by their wealth and power, control major state agencies (such as the police) and think of (black) humans as an inferior race whose purpose is to serve their whims. There are even 'Uncle Tom' humans called 'familiars', vampire wanna-bes who toady up to their vampire masters and slavishly do their bidding. Deacon Frost and his crew – most especially the ZZ-Topish vampire Quinn (Donal Logue) – are cast as white trash who enact their rage against the vampire racial hierarchy while attempting to distance themselves from their human origins by debasing and callously abusing humans. Blade then is the product of miscegenation – he is half (white) vampire and half (black) human. The interesting twist of the film is that his mixed racial derivation affords him all the strengths of the vampire with none of the weakness, except the thirst for blood, which he controls medically. In this racial allegory, the mulatto emerges as the solution to the race war between whites and blacks. Rather than one blood type overwhelming the other, the mixing of blood produces a superior race

– one that shares the white/vampire thirst for domination but recognises it as evil and controls it. Miscegenation, proposes the *Blade* films, is the answer to Western racial tension.

The third *Blade* film, *Blade: Trinity*, introduces another twist on the issues of race and racial purity that preoccupy the series as a whole: the proposition that racial purity is in fact a weakness that makes one susceptible to disease. What sets events in motion in *Blade: Trinity* is the resurrection of the ancient first vampire, Dracula (Dominic Purcell), by vampires hoping to invigorate their enervated bloodlines with his 'pure' blood. (Dracula possesses the powers to move in daylight and transform himself – powers that contemporary vampires have lost.) The vampires' emphasis on purity of blood, however, is countered by the development of a biological weapon called 'Daystar' – a virus that will kill all vampires. At the end of the film, the Daystar virus is released and presumably wipes out all vampires. Blade, however, due to his mixed blood, survives. Once again, being of mixed race is shown to be an evolutionary advantage.

In keeping with vampire movies in general, the *Blade* films are insistently about the purity of blood and bloodlines. What separates the *Blade* films from the vast majority of vampire films that precede them, however, is their attitude toward 'contamination' of blood. In the *Blade* films, purity, not contamination, is the problem. As Ann Davies (2008) observes, those vampires who seek to protect the purity of blood and bloodlines are consistently cast as villains with genocidal intentions. In contrast, the hero who possesses powers that exceed those of both vampires and humans is a mixed race hybrid. He is the synthesis that resolves the antagonism between vampires and humans – and, in these allegories of contemporary Western race relations, white and black.

The Underworld Series

The fantasy of miscegenation as the solution to contemporary racial anxieties embedded in the *Blade* films is shared and rendered even more explicitly in the *Underworld* films (*Underworld* (2003), *Underworld: Rise of the Lycans* (2006), *Underworld: Evolution* (2009)). The fundamental premise informing this series is that aristocratic vampires are at war with their former slaves, lycans (short for lycanthropes (werewolves)). It is the third film, *Underworld: Evolution*, that provides the backstory most fully: some six hundred years ago, vampires kept werewolves as slaves who performed menial labour and guarded them during the day. What touched off the race war was the forbidden romance between vampire elite, Sonja (Rhona Mitra), daughter of vampire clan elder and overlord Viktor (Bill Nighy), and werewolf slave Lucien (Michael Sheen). Rather than witness the birth of their miscegenated progeny, Viktor condemned his daughter to death by sunlight and forced Lucien to witness her transformation into ashes.

This background of racial intolerance in which a father would rather see his daughter dead than give birth to a mixed-race child provides the context for understanding the countervailing drive toward hybridity that informs the first two *Underworld* movies. In the first film, *Underworld*, Lucien's (again Sheen) objective is to end the war between vampires and lycans precisely by creating a vampire-lycan hybrid. Michael Corvin (Scott Speedman), a human descendant of the vampire/lycan common ancestor, Alexander Corvinus, becomes the film's focus because he possesses the necessary blood type to allow for this transformation. As werewolf Lucien attempts to carry out his genetic engineering experiment, agent of racial intolerance Viktor unsuccessfully races to stop him. At the end of the film, having been bitten first by Lucian and subsequently by Selene (Kate Beckinsale), Michael's transformation is complete and Viktor, champion of the old ways, is dead.

In the second *Underworld* film, *Rise of the Lycans*, it is now up to the remaining vampire elder, Marcus (Tony Curran) to restore order. He pursues Michael and Selene (Sheen and Beckinsale), but then sets his sights on liberating his twin brother William (Brian Steele), who has been locked away for the past six hundred years in a hidden fortress. Markus, the viewer learns along the way, was the first vampire; William was the first werewolf. There is a lot of fighting, but when all is said and done, both William and Markus lie dead. What survives the mayhem is Michael, the vampire/werewolf hybrid, and Selene – who, having drunk the blood of Alexander Corvinus (played by Derek Jacobi), the common ancestor of both vampires and werewolves, has become a sort of hybrid herself, able to heal and regenerate at a pace on par with Michael and to withstand the rays of the sun. With the old guard dead, Selene expects chaos within the vampire world, but ultimately is hopeful for the future and, given her romance with Michael, it seems likely that mixed race progeny is the next step in the vampire/werewolf 'evolution.'

As with the *Blade* films, the *Underworld* films clearly present an allegory of contemporary Western race relations in which the key to solving racial animosity is miscegenation. With a clear parallel to black slavery in America, *Underworld: Rise of the Lycans* shows us pasty-faced vampires making use of forced werewolf labour and decrying any possible blood rela-tion between the two races. Like some racist nineteenth-century Southern plantation owner, Viktor is so threatened and appalled by the prospect of a miscegenated child, he is willing to kill his daughter instead. But this kind of virulent racism is shown to be untenable and self-destructive in the modern age and what is revealed by the films is that vampires and werewolves are indeed derived from the same common ancestor. The prospect for resolving racial tension is shown to reside in the relationship between two 'hybrids' – Michael and Selene – whose powers exceed those of either vampires or werewolves alone.

It is very telling that the two biggest-budget and most prominent vampire action movie series of the 1990s and first decade of the twenty-first century are both oriented around questions of racial tension and share the common conceit of 'hybridity' as the solution to animosity between races. The *Blade* and *Underworld* films share with their celluloid vampire progenitors a pre-occupation with the purity of bloodlines. However, there has been a shift in polarity starting in the 1990s. Rather than the vampire being marked as racially other and figurative blackened, the vampire instead is figured as a sort of bigoted white supremacist, wed to pseudo-scientific and outdated beliefs about racial purity. Each series features a set of vampire elders who fight to preserve the status quo and refuse to acknowledge their shared relation with those they consider beneath them. Each series then demon-strates that that type of thinking has no place in the modern world and that racial mixing, rather than enervating bloodlines, in fact invigorates them.

Looking at the development of the vampire cinema, one can thus chart changing social attitudes in relation to race. From its origins to the late 1960s, whether rat-like Count Orlok or suave Count Dracula, the vampire is always a sort of dangerous ethnic invader whose bite contaminates the blood of pure white victims who then experience all sorts of perversions of decent impulses as a result. With the racial consciousness movements of the late 1960s and 1970s, the racial otherness of the vampire is explicitly acknowledged in films like *Blacula*, *Scream Blacula Scream* and *Ganja & Hess* and some measure of sympathy is allowed for the black vampire, unwillingly transformed into a monster by racist society. Then, starting in the 1990s, the implication of the idea of racialised contamination of blood is turned on its head and given a positive valence. What the Van Helsings of the vampire tradition decry and battle against is embraced in the *Blade* and *Underworld* movies as the key to progress and social harmony. Purity of blood is repeatedly associated with megalomaniacal and genocidal programmes; contamination is the key to a future of reduced racial antagonism.

Fantasies About Class

By virtue of talking about race and the *Underworld* films, we are already talking about class as well, in as much as the vampire/lycan schism divides along class lines with vampires occupying the aristocrat position and lycans forced to play the role of slave labour. The war between vampires and lycans is thus both a race war and a class war. Similarly in the *Blade* films, the vampire nation itself is hierarchically coded along class lines with 'pure blood' vampires (with European accents) at the top and 'turned' vampires portrayed as the resented and resentful nouveau riche. What these observations suggest is another core issue at the heart of the vampire film: class. In the same way that vampire films are always on various levels about sex, technology and race, they are also always about social status and class relations.

I shall develop this point briefly through attention to two films from the 1970s that consciously foreground the class rhetoric of the vampire film: *Blood for Dracula* and George A. Romero's *Martin*. *Blood for Dracula* (directed by Paul Morrissey and produced by Andy Warhol and Andrew Braunsberg) infuses the Dracula story with a comic, but acute, class consciousness. The premise of the film is that the traditionally aristocratic Count Dracula (played by Udo Kier) can only subsist on virgin blood, of which there is a severe Transylvanian shortage. Assuming that he will be more likely to find virgins in a Catholic country, he and his servant Anton (Arno Juerging) travel to Italy where they take up residence in the home of the Marchese di Fiori (Vittorio de Sica) who has fallen on hard times and who is as a result more than willing to marry off one of his four daughters to a wealthy nobleman. Also living on the estate is Mario (Joe Dallesandro), the handsome Marxist handyman who, among his other duties, sexually services the two middle daughters, Rubina (Stefania Casini) and Saphiria (Dominique Darel).

Dracula drinks the blood of Rubina and Saphiria, who are considered marriageable (the youngest, Perla (Silvia Dionisio) at fourteen is considered too young, while the eldest, Esmeralda (Milena Vukotic) is considered too plain), but since they are not virgins, their blood makes him sick. Mario, realising the danger to Perla, forces himself upon her (she is not unreceptive), ostensibly for her protection. In the meantime, however, Esmeralda has given herself to Dracula who has drunk her blood and turned her into a vampire. Mario stakes Dracula (after mostly dismembering him) and Esmeralda commits suicide by throwing herself on the stake. At the end of the film, Mario is left in charge of the estate.

Principally a campy sex romp, *Blood for Dracula* initially received an X rating when released in theatres in America due to its sexual and violent elements. It was subsequently re-edited and received an R rating for re-release. Part of the humour of the film, however, depends upon its parodic rendering of the conventional class identifications of the vampire film. Dracula in *Blood for Dracula* is Dracula on life-support – a parodic rendering of the enervated, debased aristocrat who has survived off the life's blood of the peasantry but is unable to thrive in a modern world in which not only sexual values have changed, but the aristocracy no longer commands the automatic obedience of the working class. Mario, in turn, is himself a parody of the Marxist revolutionary who refuses to accept the traditional social hierarchy; in essence, he enacts his own mini-revolution, vanquishing the despotic aristocrat and taking control of the means of production at the end. What *Blood for Dracula* reveals is that the vampire mythos is based around an exploitative class relation in which upper class drains the working class.

The deviation that proves this rule most clearly is Romero's *Martin*, one of the very few vampire movies – and likely the first – to feature a working class vampire. Latham writes that, in the history of the vampire cinema, there have been few such figures, 'largely because the vampire's superior strength, extended life span, and hypnotic powers of mind control usually facilitate the amassing of wealth and servants'; he continues, 'Indeed, these supernatural gifts tend to provide an alternative mechanism of economic enfranchisement to the conventional hierarchies of class origin or the promised fruits of hard work, making the vampire an upwardly mobile identity almost by definition' (2002: 76). Latham's observations are correct, but one also needs to bear in mind the use of the vampire by nineteenth-century Romanticists as a metaphor for a debased aristocracy living off the labour of the peasantry. As McClelland points out in *Slayers and Their Vampires*,

Romanticists such as Byron, Polidori, LeFanu and others allegorised the vampire (who, interestingly, is not an aristocrat in European folklore, but part of the general population) as representative of the 'growing economic disparity between social classes' (2006: 150). This suggests that in the beginning, there was the aristocratic vampire and explanations for his status – superior strength, extended life span, and so forth – came later.

Martin, in Kim Newman's estimation 'the most thoroughgoing, sophisticated re-examination of the vampire figure yet attempted' (1988: 30), does not follow the 'vampire formula'. Martin (John Amplas) is not sexy, aristocratic or commanding – indeed, he may not even be a vampire at all, and this is the film's real complication. Despite Martin's monochromatic flashbacks to a romanticised vampire past in which he feeds on a beautiful woman in a mansion and is chased through the streets by peasants with torches, there is nothing supernatural about Martin (he lacks fangs and instead sedates his victims with hypodermic needles before cutting them with razor blades, he does not transform, he is not bothered by crosses or garlic, and so forth) and nothing to confirm Tata Cuda's (Lincoln Maazel) accusations that Martin is an 84-year-old vampire with European origins or Martin's own assertions to a radio talk-show host (Michael Gornick) about his vampirism.

For Latham, *Martin*, which is set in the town of Braddock, Pennsylvania – an economically-depressed suburb of Pittsburgh marked by unemployment and poverty – is a 'meditation on deindustrialization and the social marginalisation of working-class youth' (2002: 81) that exemplifies the conflicted post-Fordist construction of youth: 'Martin's personal "sickness" is itself a symptom of the malaise of a system that conceives only one role for youth – the idleness and hedonism of consumption – but then indicts young people for enacting it' (2002: 74). Latham in fact sees *Martin* as pioneering the figure of the 'slacker', a social identity that achieved cultural prominence in the 1980s. Abbott similarly interprets *Martin* as documenting the 1970s American transformation from an industrial to a post-industrial economy and cultural anxieties concerning youth 'raised in a dying industrial landscape with no prospects' (2007: 94). *Martin*, in Abbott's opinion, 'Americanizes' the vampire and updates it to reflect the socio-economic realities of the period.

These assessments by Latham and Abbott foreground the ways in which *Martin* is a vampire film about the economic realities of 1970s America. But what *Martin* highlights through its rescripting of the vampire as a working-class twenty-something going through the motions in an economically depressed post-industrial town is the basic premise that the dread and desire associated with the vampire is always inextricably interconnected with his class location. *Martin*, by consciously breaking with the traditions of the vampire cinema, makes those traditions – the formula – clearly evident. Indeed, Martin's (real or imagined) flashbacks to his European vampire past in which he was both aristocratic and hunted by the peasantry force the viewer to mark the break the film enacts with the vampire cinema's past. *Martin* is the exception that proves the rule – the vampire cinema as a genre is undergirded by a discourse about social class.

Race, Class and Religion – The Breed

Much of the preceding discussion is encapsulated by one of the more interesting and lesser-known vampire films of the first decade of the twenty-first century, *The Breed*. Indeed, the film constitutes a veritable bricolage of themes, allusions and images as it appropriates and redeploys elements from the vampire cinematic and literary traditions, as well as the action, fantasy, science fiction and film noir movie genres more generally. Set in an odd dystopic 'near future', *The Breed*, borrowing freely from Terry Gilliam's fantasy classic, *Brazil* (1985), eclectically combines 1940s American culture with contemporary aspects and futuristic technology. After a strange series of murders, including one in which his partner is killed by an assailant with seemingly supernatural powers, hard-boiled black detective Stephen Grant (Bokeem Woodbine) is called in by the fascistic National Security Agency to investigate and is assigned a partner, vampire Aaron Gray (Adrian Paul of *Highlander: The Series* fame). What is revealed to Grant, who previously was unaware of the existence of vampires, is that vampires are a genetic 'offshoot' of humanity, a 'different kind of breed', and that there are about four thousand of them worldwide. Sounding quite a lot like the situation in the recent Home Box Office (HBO) series *True Blood*, the vampires have recently 'come out of the closet' to the government, as the minor character, Dean Fusco (William Hootkins) puts it, and revealed themselves voluntarily to humanity with the hope that the two races can peacefully coexist. Not all vampires, however, wish this plan to succeed and the initial speculation is that the murders may be politically motivated – a vampire attempt to scuttle the integrationist plan. Distrust, however, exists on both sides. What is revealed to Grant by his superiors is that the NSA's Dr Fleming (James Booth) has developed a contagious airborne virus that, while only causing minor illness in humans, impacts vampires like the Ebola virus (decidedly worse than the Swine Flu!) and has the potential to wipe them out completely.

With the assistance of Asian vampire Lucy Westenra (Ling Bai), who becomes Grant's lover, Grant and Gray seem to uncover a vampire resistance plot to import weapons and Grant sets up a government sting operation. It turns out, however, that rather than weapons being imported into the country, vampire emigrants, fearing governmental persecution, are being smuggled out; when government forces open fire on the vampire emigrants and their guards, ignoring Grant's explicit instructions to wait for his orders, Grant is put in the difficult position of defending the vampires and firing back upon his own government's troops.

What Grant and Gray ultimately discover is that the murders and their investigation have been orchestrated by the vampire mastermind, the ironically-named Friedrich Cross (Péter Halász), to inflame human passions to the point at which the anti-vampire virus is released. This is because, unknown to the NSA, Dr Fleming has made an arrangement with Cross to alter the virus such that it impacts *humans* rather than vampires in exchange for being turned into a vampire. Cross's vision is to overcome the race problem by unleashing the virus and then to save humanity through infusions of vampire blood that will in effect create one race. Working together, Grant and Gray uncover and thwart the plot and the film ends with them as permanent partners and with Grant solidifying his relationship with vampire Lucy.

The Breed, while in many ways a flawed movie (there are holes in the plot, the noir-ish dialogue sometimes comes off as just stilted, the *Matrix*-influenced fight scenes look more silly than cool), is nonetheless fascinating as a sort of vampire action film nexus that both draws upon the existing tradition and seems to predict future developments. The film as vampire cinema homage is readily apparent, for example, in an early scene in which Grant and Gray are called to 'the Freudian Building', owned by psychologist Graf Orlock (István Göz), to investigate the serial killer's latest victim, a student named Barbara Steele. Graf (German for Count) Orlok is of course the vampire in *Nosferatu*, while Barbara Steele is the name of the actress who famously starred in a number of horror movies, including the excellent vampire movies *Black Sunday* (1960) and *Castle of Blood* (1964). Referencing the action genre more generally, Dr Fleming tells Grant that Grant is no James Bond and he is no Blofeld – Ian Fleming was the author of the James Bond novels and Blofeld (most famously played by Charles Gray) is among Bond's primary nemeses. Indeed, these sorts of conscious puns and allusions are everywhere in the film: borrowing from Bram Stoker, one of the NSA higher-ups is named Seward (Lo Ming), while Lucy Westenra is ironically featured as a vampire (a conceit also utilised by *The League of Extraordinary Gentlemen*). Another NSA employee who conducts an autopsy at the start of the film on Grant's partner is named Bathory (Debbie Javor), while the founder of the vampire community (named 'Serenity') is, as noted, ironically named Cross. Throughout the film, vampires in 'reality' are contrasted with those in film and at one point a minor character putting on airs is told to 'quit the Anne Rice routine'.

On an even more general level, the film clearly draws upon and amalgamates a range of influences – and in interesting ways seems itself to have influenced the overall vampire cinema zeitgeist. In terms of setting and general aesthetic, the film combines the anachronistic temporality and eclectic dystopianism of Terry Gilliam's *Brazil* with the science fiction/film noir synthesis of *Dark City* (1998). The acrobatic fight scenes, the idea of vampires subsisting on a blood substitute, and one scene shot in a vampire nightclub all seem directly appropriated from *Blade*, while curiously the idea of contending viruses that kill humans or vampires becomes the premise of *Blade: Trinity*. As noted above, the premise of vampires 'coming out of the closet' and revealing their existence to humanity is the structuring conceit of the HBO series *True Blood* – as is the idea of vampires subsisting on a blood substitute (a premise underlying the sf grade 'B' vampire film, *Vampirella*, as well as the *Blade* franchise).

In these ways, I think one needs to think of *The Breed* as a sort of 'metamovie', a film about vampire films and their relation to cinematic genres. Indeed, I suspect the film performed poorly at the box office because, like a vampire that derives sustenance from multiple victims, *The Breed* is a film that schizophrenically attempts to incorporate elements of the horror, sf, fantasy, mystery, film noir and action genres into one unwieldy body. As I will discuss in the Coda that follows, the continued success of the vampire cinema has to do precisely with the vampire's monstrous ability to colonise other genres – unlike most other cinematic monsters, the vampire's protean abilities allows it to move more or less fluidly from one generic context to the next. *The Breed* demonstrates this vampiric tendency to cannibalise other genres, even if its sutures perhaps show too much.

Where the film does riff on an established vampire cinema theme in a new and interesting way is through its paralleling the vampire population with Jews and reversing the vampiric polarity such that the vampires constitute an oppressed minority. As I've discussed throughout this chapter, the vampire in twentieth-century cinema generally acts as a sort of generic metaphor for social otherness or outsiderdom. Thus, the overdetermined vampire is the foreign invader, the sexual deviant, the voracious capitalist exploiting the poor, the insidious communist who would sap our independence and individuality, and so forth. Given the ease with which the vampire metaphor can be adapted to participate in the demonisation of social minorities, it is not surprising that anti-Semitic rhetoric would associate Jews and vampires and, indeed, as McClelland has discussed in his 'deep history' of the vampire, the term *vampir*, which originated in the eastern Balkans somewhere between eight hundred and a thousand years ago, drew together 'the triad of Jews, pagans, and heretics that together coalesced into the image of the enemy of Christianity' (2006: 7; 47). In another context, I have discussed historical connections between anti-Semitic myths and vampires, including the 'blood libel' – the charge that Jews murder Christian children and drink their blood – as well as charges that Jews spread disease. Of course, the familiar anti-Semitic metaphor of the 'blood-sucking' money-lending Jew still perniciously circulates in contemporary culture.

Both the vampire literary and film traditions have on various levels drawn upon the anti-Semitic associations of the vampire. Thus, in Stoker's *Dracula*, Dracula's escape from England is aided by Immanuel Hildesheim, 'a Hebrew of the rather Alephi type, with a nose like a sheep, and a fez' (see McClelland 2006: 302), a point which leads Ken Gelder to conclude that 'the anti-Semitic mythology of the Eastern European Jew folded in to what became – through Stoker's novel – the "Dracula myth"' (1994: 16). Murnau's *Nosferatu* has been noted by a number of commentators as deploying anti-Semitic stereotypes through its paralleling of the plague-spreading vampire, Count Orlock, with Jews – the deformed 'property-acquiring Jew-vampire' (Gelder 1994: 96) invades German borders and spreads disease and death in its wake. While few vampire films are as open in demonising

Jews as, say, homosexuals, the anti-Semitic undercurrents are never far from the surface in films in which crosses function as prophylactics, vampires are the enemies of God, and vampires suck the blood of Christians. (Interestingly, the only explicitly Jewish vampires that I've come across are in comedies – *Fearless Vampire Killers* and *A Polish Vampire in Burbank* (1985). The possible exception here is Clive Barker's recent vampire trilogy, *Dracula 2000*, *Dracula II: Ascension* (2003) and *Dracula III: Legacy* (2005), in which it is revealed that Dracula is in fact Judas himself, cursed by God for his role in Jesus' crucifixion. As Judas, Dracula would have been Jewish; Jewish religious iconography or symbolism is absent from the films however.)

The Breed draws upon this legacy of anti-Semitism when it characterises vampires as Jews. It then turns this anti-Semitic vampire cinema tradition on its head by identifying vampires as an oppressed minority subject to discrimination and potential extermination by a state-sanctioned genocidal programme. This identification is done in two ways: first, detective Aaron Gray is himself Jewish. Initially through a sequence of brief flashbacks and then through Gray's narration to Grant, the viewer learns that Gray was a Polish Jew who escaped into the woods with his wife and daughter when the Nazis invaded their town. Although they avoided the Nazis, they could not escape the cold and his wife and daughter froze to death before Gray encountered Cross, who turned him into a vampire. Gray then walked into the nearby Nazi encampment to wreak an especially bloody form of revenge.

Beyond explicitly identifying Gray as Jewish, the film in a variety of ways visually equates vampires with Jews. The vampires, living in a fascist state that has been working toward developing a vampire 'final solution', are ghettoised in an encampment ironically named 'Serenity'. Subject to anti-vampire sentiments from the bulk of the vampirophobes who know of their existence (including Grant at the start of the film), they are represented as poor immigrants, dressed in 1930s/1940s-style clothing that would not be out of place in the Don Corleone flashback sequences of *The Godfather II* (1974). Most tellingly, the innocent vampires are attacked by government troops while attempting to sneak out of the country.

The Breed thus enacts a series of generic inversions that clearly correlate vampires with social outsiderdom and then, rather than expelling the other as a threat to social stability, foregrounds the injustice of bigotry and intolerance. Intolerance of social difference in fact becomes a primary theme of the film as various vampires remind bigoted humans of the violence humans have done to one another. The vampire resistance leader Vladimir de Torquemada West (Zen Gesner) opposes vampires revealing their existence to humans because he has 'seen slavery, witch hunts, the massacre of millions of Jews'. Similarly, Cross justifies his plan to infect humanity with the engineered virus that only vampire blood can cure because he has seen what human beings have done to Indians, Africans and Jews. Indeed, the entire film is based around the difficulties of vampire/human coexistence as the vampires debate the best course of action to combat hatred of vampires.

As discussed above, using the vampire as a metaphor for a minority group as a way to engage obliquely with issues of social tension in relation to race, class, sexuality and religion has become an increasingly prominent device in post-1960s vampire films. *The Breed*, however, is a breed apart from both the blaxploitation films of the 1970s and the vampire action films of the 1990s and the first decade of the twenty-first century in raising issues of race without either demonising the racial other or proposing miscegenation as the solution to contemporary racial tension. In the two *Blacula* films, Blacula – while a product of victimisation and the slave trade – remains at least part monster and the trajectory of each film is toward his destruction. Similarly, Dr Green in *Ganja & Hess* is shown in various ways to be preying upon his own people and is gone at the end of the film (although Ganja remains). In *The Breed*, however, the vampires for the most part are presented sympathetically – as an oppressed minority more fearful than feared. Although the vampire Cross hatches a plan to infect humanity with a dangerous virus, the plan horrifies both humans and other vampires and in the end he is thwarted by human/vampire cooperation. In keeping with contemporary awareness of the ways in which minority populations have been victimised by those in power, *The Breed* in fact is far more critical of the white fascistic power structure than it is of the vampires.

Tolerance of difference is thus the underlying theme of *The Breed*. What is explicitly rejected by the film, however, is the affirmation of miscegenation as the key to achieving racial parity by scuttling categorisational rubrics. The film in fact rejects this approach in two ways. First, as mentioned above, Dr Cross's plan for a forced integration of vampires and humans by creating a virulent virus that can only be cured by infusing vampire blood into humans is presented as monstrous and is stopped. Second, the black detective Grant is revealed to be among the twenty percent of the human population 'immune' to vampire transformation – which means that Lucy cannot transform her lover into an immortal companion. What the film ends with is a black human engaged in a romantic relationship with an Asian vampire (with a castle and a pet panther no less!) and with a Polish-Jewish vampire police partner – which is to say a multicultural vision of harmonious coexistence and respect for differences.

The Breed is, as I have suggested, a kind of node on the distributed vampire network – a film built out of the bits and pieces of the vampire tradition that (not always successfully) appropriates and incorporates various allusions, motifs and themes of the vampire film and other generic traditions. But through its explicit paralleling of vampires and Jews as oppressed minorities subject to the brutality of a culture intolerant of difference, it clearly illustrates the central theme of this chapter – the way in which the vampire film is always undergirded by ideas of social conformity and alienation, of belonging and outsiderdom. In the same way in which any discussion of the vampire inevitably intersects with understandings of sex and technology, the vampire is always marked by his social difference, be it ethic, ideological or religious – or more properly an overdetermined combination.

What differentiates contemporary vampire films most vividly from pre-1970s films is the attitude toward difference conveyed by the films. While the conventional vampire plot in which the vampire is an alien invader that needs to be destroyed remains common (witness *30 Days of Night*, in which vampires are monsters with their own language), modern films – in keeping with modern emphases on tolerance and the value of cultural diversity – increasingly reverse the *Nosferatu* polarity and recast the vampire not as villain, but as hero. This trend, evident in *The Breed* and the *Underworld* and *Blade* films, is also evident in the *Buffy the Vampire Slayer* TV spin-off, *Angel*, as well as in *True Blood*, and is at the centre of both *Twilight* and *Let the Right One In*. But whichever way the compass points – be it toward good or evil – the vampire is always the other, defined by his or her difference from the rank and file of common humanity.

CODA: VAMPIRISING GENRE

Vampires are no respecters of boundaries. As one might expect from monsters immune to the ravages of time and constantly in need of fresh blood, cinematic vampires have spread out all over the world and are to be found in the unlikeliest of places. Consider for example a high point in silly movies: *Billy the Kid vs. Dracula*. In this sublimely ridiculous film, Dracula, played by veteran horror movie actor John Carradine, has relocated to the old West and seeks to convert Billy the Kid's (Chuck Courtney) lovely, ranch-owning fiancée, Betty (Melinda Plowman), into his vampire bride. The obligatory mayhem ensues and the film culminates in an abandoned mine where, after his bullets have no effect, Billy the Kid throws his gun at Dracula and it surprisingly knocks him out cold. Billy then stakes Dracula and the viewer is treated to a delightfully fake rubber bat emerging out of the mine into bright daylight and then falling 'dead' to the earth.

Yes, *Billy the Kid vs. Dracula* is a ridiculous film, but the writers of the videogame-based *BloodRayne II: Deliverance* must have paid careful attention because in this Old West epic, Dracula *is* Billy the Kid. When 700-year-old Transylvanian vampire Billy the Kid (Zack Ward) comes calling to the quiet Old West town of Deliverance, interestingly intending to make it a railroad hub and then to use it to create a vampire army and send them out across the country, it is up to sexy half-vampire (or *dhampir*) Rayne (Natassia Malthe) and her makeshift posse of vampire hunters to stop him with swords, pistols and a Gatling gun from taking over America.

Perhaps given the draftiness of medieval Transylvanian castles, one should not be surprised to find vampires in warmer climates. California, after all, as depicted by the vampire cinema, has been overrun with vampires, with Los Angeles in particular as a kind of vampire earthquake epicenter. To Abbott's list of *Fright Night, Fright Night Part II, The Lost Boys, Beverly Hills Vamp* (1989), *Buffy the Vampire Slayer, Blood Ties* and *Blade*, one could also add a number of other vampire films set in LA, including the two Blacula movies, the two Count Yorga movies (*Count Yorga, Vampire* (1970) and *The Return of Count Yorga* (1971)) and *Dance of the Damned* (1988). Lurking in the desert outside LA is seductive vampire Diane LeFanu (Celeste Yarnall) in *The Velvet Vampire* (1971), while the New Mexico desert is home to a clutch of vampires in *John Carpenter's Vampires*.

Occasionally in a form of reverse immigration the vampire emigrates south from LA to Mexico. In *El Vampiro*, a Mexican film sometimes referred to as 'Dracula on the hacienda' (and the first film to represent the vampire with elongated canines since *Nosferatu*), the vampire, Count Karol de Lavud (Germán Robles) (cleverly concealing his identity in his day-to-day interactions with his neighbours by calling himself Duval, Lavud spelled backwards – a convention itself borrowed from *Son of Dracula* (1943) featuring Lon Chaney Jr as Count Alucard), covets a neighbouring ranch (a premise appropriated, one might note, by *Billy the Kid vs. Dracula!*). The vampire in *El Vampiro* engages in the usual shenanigans and then is dispatched in the usual way, but Mexican vampires sometimes require more unorthodox policing – as witnessed by the series of vampire wrestling films based around masked wrestler Santo. Mexican vampires are particularly nasty in the Robert Rodriquez/Quentin Tarrantino production, *From Dusk Till Dawn* (as well as its straight-to-video sequels, *From Dusk Till Dawn 2: Texas Blood Money* (1999) and *From Dusk Till Dawn 3: The Hangman's Daughter* (2000)).

While vampires frequently seem to seek warmer temperatures to take the chill off of their undead bones, they in some cases stalk frozen landscapes as well. In the cinematic adaptation of the graphic novel *30 Days of Night*, vampires logically invade the Alaskan town of Barrow (north of the Arctic Circle) because what better hunting ground is there for vampires immune to cold than a place that, in winter, experiences a month of darkness? The vampire Eli in *Let the Right One In* also benefits from the prolonged darkness of winter, this time in Sweden (vampires in this film literally burst into flame when they come in contact with sunlight), and coldness is almost tangible in vampire films including the 'Wurdalak' section of

Mario Bava's *Black Sabbath* (1963), Polanski's *The Fearless Vampire Killers*, Cronenberg's *Rabid*, *Van Helsing* and *Frostbitten* (2006).

Whether they head south or north, vampires, it seems, just cannot stay put in Transylvania – and their predations are not limited solely to the Old and New Worlds. Both in terms of settings within films and the production of vampire films themselves, the vampire is a global phenomenon. For example, in the Japanese production *Lake of Dracula* (1971), the vampire is exported to Japan. Dracula travels to China in the Hammer Studios kung-fu vampire hybrid, *The Legend of the 7 Golden Vampires*, and Wesley Snipes' vampire hero Blade roots out nasty Russian vampires in *Blade II* – Russia is also plagued by vampires in the very interesting Russian *Night Watch* and *Day Watch* films. Vampires in India are the problem in *Bandh Darwaza* (1990), while the backstory to *Ganja & Hess* involves an African vampire tribe. Nomadic vampires roam from place to place in a variety of films including *Near Dark*, *Habit* and *The Forsaken* and vampires can be found all around the world in any number of vampire films from *The Last Man on Earth* to *Underworld* and *Blade* films. Vampires are not even confined to this planet – while there are no actual vampires in Mario Bava's *Planet of the Vampires* (1965), intergalactic vampires are the problem in films including *Planet of Blood*, *Lifeforce* and *Vampirella*.

In short, cinematic vampires are constantly on the move and can now be found everywhere. They can be urban (*Wisdom of Crocodiles* (1998), *Habit*), suburban (*My Best Friend is a Vampire* (1988), *Buffy the Vampire Slayer*), or rural (*Vampires Anonymous* (2000), *Bloodsucking Redneck Vampires* (2004)). Although stereotypically found in castles, you can find them in mansions (*Blood and Roses* (1960), *Vampyres* (1974)), condos (*Vampire's Kiss* (1988)), boats (*Habit*) or vans (*Near Dark*). Although most often creatures of a romanticised past, they stalk the present as well (*Embrace of the Vampire* (1994), *The Addiction* (1995)), and occasionally are thrust into the science fictive future (*Ultraviolet* (2006), *Dracula 3000* (2004)).

Super-Genre

But vampires spread out in more ways than one. Beyond geographic distribution – both in terms of cinematic setting and cinematic production – what distinguishes the vampire film is its colonisation (or vampirisation) of various genres. In addition to blood-drenched vampire horror films, there are vampire comedies, westerns, love stories, action films, road movies, kung-fu films, space operas, ballets (*Dracula: Pages From a Virgin's Diary* (2002)), and – if one is willing to accept a 'sweet transvestite from Transsexual Transylvania' as a sort of sexual vampire (*The Rocky Horror Picture Show* (1975)) – the musical as well. Vampire films can be absurdly poor 'B' films, general release blockbusters or art-house films. And the vampire him- or herself can be hero, antihero or villain; protagonist or antagonist. In short, the only thing that absolutely defines a vampire film is the presence of an entity that either drinks blood or, more loosely, in some way 'drains' the life-force of someone or something else. Vampire films thus cannot be construed as constituting any kind of coherent genre.

One hastens to add here that while the presence of a blood- or life-sucker is all that is required to categorise a movie as a vampire film, vampire films are arguably unique in being defined in relation to a single primary Ur-text: Bram Stoker's novel *Dracula*. That is, Stoker's Dracula is the vampire representation that sets the vampire norm and to which all other vampire representations inevitably are compared. Indeed, Stoker's vampire has so seeped into the collective unconscious that even those who have never read the novel or seen a vampire film can still list the vampire's primary defining characteristics: subsists on blood, sleeps in a coffin, warded off by crosses and garlic, lacks a reflection, can transform into a bat, killed by staking. Over top of this basic characterisation, a secondary set of defining characteristics, primarily traceable to the Universal Studios horror movie cycle of the 1930s and 1940s – most especially *Dracula* from 1931 with Bela Lugosi which can be considered the cinematic vampire ur-text – but also the Hammer Studios films of the 1960s and 1970s, has been added: aristocratic bearing, 'exotic' accent, black cape, severely allergic to sunlight, mesmeric gaze.

What this suggests is that at this point, we are all inevitably, to borrow from Henry Jenkins, vampire textual nomads. We cannot consume any vampire media, be it cinematic, televisual, literary, theatrical, musical or even play a video game featuring vampires without consciously or unconsciously relating the new representation to the vampire 'super genre' – Stoker's Ur-text, Bela Lugosi's Dracula, and all subsequent homages and deviations. All new vampire representations in various ways not only ask but indeed demand that the spectator-as-critic engage in a process of comparison in order to acknowledge both what is new and what is conventional. This allows the spectator then to recognise what is an original innovation (say, giving vampires a glittering aura, relating them to werewolves, having them originate in Africa, or identifying the cause of vampirism as a mechanical scarab-like device), what is 'faithful' to the vampire's literary and cinematic origins, and what is somewhere between the two, such as Dracula being paralysed by a cross made by holding two candle sticks perpendicular (*The Horror of Dracula*) or destroyed by the cross made by the shadow of a windmill (*The Brides of Dracula* (1960)).

Beyond this, what clearly marks contemporary vampire narratives of all stripes is not just the insistence upon the audience's intertextual nomadic consciousness, but the metatextual awareness of the films themselves. All vampire movies after Tod Browning's *Dracula* are on some level aware of themselves as vampire movies attempting to depart from yet remain close to the conventions established by Stoker and Browning. Vampire movies are thus always about vampire movies. This is somewhat different from my assertion in Chapter Two that vampire movies are always on some level about the magic making of the cinema itself. There I was arguing that vampires as creations of the cinema always in a variety of ways are related to and foreground the technology of cinema. Here I am suggesting that vampire movies always define themselves in relation to previous cinematic representations of vampires and often are quite explicit about the revisions to the mythology that they are making. This is most readily apparent in films in which the protagonists refer to the vampire tradition in order to devise strategies of resistance to the vampire and/or in films in which the vampire him- or herself explicitly contrasts his abilities in relation to other representations (these features often go together). For example, in *The Lost Boys*, Edgar (Corey Feldman) and Alan (Jamison Newlander) are aware that vampires are afoot in Santa Carla because of their consumption of vampire comic books and are able to develop effective means of confronting the vampire because of this knowledge. In *'Salem's Lot*, protagonist Mark Petrie (Lance Kerwin) also comes supplied with this knowledge while protagonists Ben Mears (David Soul) and Jason Burke (Lou Ayres) find themselves resorting to Stoker and other literary representations of vampires to devise ways to confront the vampire Barlow. More recently – and comically – the vampire Count Orlok in *Shadow of the Vampire* discusses his response to Stoker's *Dracula*: it made him sad to think of Count Dracula being reduced to having to cater to Jonathan Harker's needs (making the bed, preparing a meal).

Blade: Trinity similarly offers an explicit comparison between Dracula as introduced in the film (a six-to-seven-thousand-year-old monster emerging from ancient Sumeria) and Stoker's creation.

In an ironic way, part of what allows vampires so easily to colonise various genres is arguably our ready conversance with the vampire Ur-texts – Stoker's novel and Lugosi's portrayal. What allows us to recognise the originality of the retelling is our familiarity with the canonical texts. The challenge to filmmakers then is to tell a familiar story in a new way, to take something well-worn and cherished and reinvent it in an original fashion. The meta-textual awareness of most contemporary vampire films is acknowledgment of this objective. It is the attempt to make clear even to the most obtuse or culturally unaware of viewers that the film and its makers are cognisant of the tradition and have attempted – for better or for worse – to reimagine it. But the challenge to filmmakers to do something original with a familiar tale is insufficient to explain the prolificness and diversity of vampire films. In the preceding chapters, I have argued that the enduring appeal of vampire films is related to their essential engagement with three broad themes: sex, technology and cultural otherness. In closing here, I would like to address one final theme that transcends genre and helps to explain the vampire's ubiquity: the power dynamic inherent in draining and being drained of life.

As I mention above, beyond all the conventional trappings of the vampire film, what makes a vampire a vampire is, as Mary Pharr (1999) observes, appetite and the act of sucking. This can be the crude consumption of blood or the metaphorical draining of energy or life-force, as in *A Fool There Was*, Franco's soft-core pornographic *Female Vampire* in which the vampire Countess Irina von Karstein (Lina Romay) subsists off the release of energy coincident with the male orgasm, or even arguably *The Red Violin* (1998), in which a masterpiece of musical technology, a violin varnished with a dead woman's blood, progressively takes over the lives of a variety of owners. The actual draining of blood of course characterises the literal vampire. But blood is never just blood, never just liquid. Rather it constitutes one of the most powerful and universally acknowledged human symbols – as Stoker's Renfield wisely, if cryptically, intones: 'For the blood is the life' (1997: 206). The taking or surrendering of blood or life-force thus participates in a complicated dynamic of power and submission.

From this observation, two conclusions can be drawn that help to explain the endless fascination the vampire exerts and the ease with which the vampire spreads out and subsumes cinematic genre: first, the allure of the vampire is related to his or her power over life and death. Second, the vampire is always already a metaphor. The vampire's control over life and death functions in two ways. To begin with, the vampire is by definition 'undead' – it itself is an entity that subsists beyond its literal death. It is horrific by virtue of being liminal in the sense famously developed by anthropologist Mary Douglass in *Purity and Danger* (1966), as well as by Jeffrey Jerome Cohen in *Monster Theory* (1996), that is, in transgressing categorical distinctions; at the same time, however, it fascinates. It is the thing that has died and come back, that has defied humankind's greatest fear. In addition, the vampire in both literature and cinema has come to symbolise power over the lives of others. The vampire mesmerises its victims, saps them of their will, and enslaves them. It subsists off of the life-force of other people, subjecting them to its desires and controlling their fates. Not only has the vampire conquered death, but it controls the lives and deaths of others. Its power is both alluring and terrifying – and, to repeat a point introduced at the start – the vampire is as a result always more interesting than those who pursue it.

The vampire thus comes already prepackaged as a symbol of control over life and death and added to this is the ready symbolism of the taking of blood. As I have suggested above, blood is never just blood; it is life itself. Thus, the vampire's draining of blood symbolises the exertion of its control over the lives of others. The combination of the two – the powerful force or entity that defies death through draining the life of others – yields a terrifically potent and endlessly malleable combination. The vampire thus is always already a sort of dictator and obsession and addiction that both seduces and repels in equal measure. And when this power dynamic is inserted into a particular cultural context and sexualised, technologised and othered, what emerges is a supercharged, overdetermined surplus of meaning – a symbolic supertext operating on multiple levels simultaneously. It is not then that, as David Pirie (1977) would have it, America – or the world for that matter – always gets the vampire it deserves; but rather, it is the vampire that always gets us.

FILMOGRAPHY

30 Days of Night (David Slade, 2007, US)

Addiction, The (Abel Ferarra, 1995, US)

A Fool There Was (Frank Powell, 1915, US)

A Polish Vampire in Burbank (Mark Pirro, 1985, US)

A Trip to the Moon [Le voyage dans la lune] (Georges Méliès, 1902, France)

Austin Powers: International Man of Mystery (Jay Roach, 1997, US)

Bandh Darwaza (Shyam Ramsay and Tulsi Ramsay, 1990, India)

Batman (Tim Burton, 1989, US)

Beauty and the Beast [La belle et la bête] (Jean Cocteau, 1946, France)

Beverly Hills Vamp (Fred Olen Ray, 1989, US)

Billy the Kid vs. Dracula (William Beaudine, 1966, US)

Black Sabbath [I tre volti della paura] (Mario Bava, 1963, Italy)

Black Sunday [La maschera del demonio] (Mario Bava, 1961, Italy)

Blacula (William Crain, 1972, US)

Blade (Stephen Norrington, 1998, US)

Blade II (Guillermo del Toro, 2002, US)

Blade: Trinity (David S. Goyer, 2004, US)

Blood and Roses [Et mourir de plaisir] (Roger Vadim, 1960, France)

Blood for Dracula [Dracula cerca sangue di vergine... e morì di sete!!!]
     (Paul Morrissey, 1974, Italy)

Bloodrayne II: Deliverance (Uwe Boll, 2007, Canada)

Bloodsucking Redneck Vampires (Mike Hegg and Joe Sherlock, 2004, US)

Blood Ties (Jim McBride, 1991, US)

Bram Stoker's Dracula (Francis Ford Coppola, 1992, US)

Brazil (Terry Gilliam, 1985, UK)

Breed, The (Michael Oblowitz, 2001, US)

Brides of Dracula (Terence Fisher, 1960, UK)

Bubba Ho-tep (Don Coscarelli, 2002, US)
Buffy the Vampire Layer (Jack Stephen, 1996, US)
Buffy the Vampire Slayer (Fran Rubel Kuzui, 1992, US)
Captain Kronos—Vampire Hunter (Brian Clemens, 1994, UK)
Castle of Blood [*Danza macabra*] (Antonio Margheriti, 1964, Italy)
Count Yorga, Vampire (Bob Kelljan, 1970, US)
Cronos (Guillermo del Toro, 1993, Mexico)
Crypt of the Vampire [*La cripta e l'incubo*] (Camillo Mastrocinque, 1964, Italy)
Curse of the Undead (Edward Dein, 1959, US)
Dance of the Damned (Katt Shea, 1988, US)
Dance of the Vampires. See: *Fearless Vampire Killers.*
Dark City (Alex Proyas, 1998, Australia)
Daughters of Darkness [*Les lèvres rouges*] (Harry Kümel, 1971, Belgium)
Dawn of the Dead (George A. Romero, 1978, Italy/US)
Day Watch [*Dnevnoy dozor*] (Timur Bekmambetov, 2006, Russia)
Die Hard (John McTiernan, 1988, US)
Dracula (Tod Browning, 1931, US)
Dracula (John Badham, 1979, US/UK)
Dracula 2000 (Patrick Lussier, 2000, US)
Dracula 3000 (Darrell Roodt, 2004, US)
Dracula II: Ascension (Patrick Lussier, 2003, US)
Dracula III: Legacy (Patrick Lussier, 2005, US)
Dracula's Daughter. (Lambert Hillyer, 1936, US)
Dracula: Dead and Loving It (Mel Brooks, 1995, US)
Dracula: Pages From a Virgin's Diary (Guy Maddin, 2002, Canada)
Ejacula, la Vampira (Alessandro del Mar, 1992, Italy)
El Vampiro (Fernando Méndez, 1957, Mexico)
Embrace of the Vampire (Anne Goursaud,1995, US)
Encounters of the Spooky Kind [*Gui da gui*] (Sammo Hung Kam-Bo, 1980, Hong Kong)
English Patient, The (Anthony Minghella, 1996, US/UK)
Fearless Vampire Killers or: Pardon Me, But Your Teeth Are in My Neck (Roman Polanski, 1967, US/UK)
Female Vampire [*Les avaleuses*] (Jesús Franco, France, 1973)
Forsaken, The (J. S. Cardone, 2001, US)
Fright Night (Tom Holland, 1985, US)
Fright Night Part 2 (Tommy Lee Wallace, 1988, US)
From Dusk Till Dawn (Robert Rodriguez, 1996, US)
From Dusk Till Dawn 2: Texas Blood Money (Scott Spiegel, 1999, US)
From Dusk Till Dawn 3: The Hangman's Daughter (P. J. Pesce, 2000, US)

Frostbitten (Anders Banke, 2006, Sweden).
Ganja & Hess (Bill Gunn, 1973, US)
Godfather: Part II, The (Francis Ford Coppola, 1974, US)
Habit (Larry Fessenden, 1997, US)
Horror of Dracula (Terrence Fisher, 1985, UK)
Hunger, The (Tony Scott, 1983, UK)
I Am Legend (Francis Lawrence, 2007, US)
Innocent Blood (John Landis, 1992, US)
Interview With the Vampire (Neil Jordan, 1994, US)
Invasion of the Body Snatchers, The (Don Siegel, 1956, US)
Jesus Christ Vampire Hunter (Lee Demarbre, 2001, Canada)
John Carpenter's Vampires (John Carpenter, 1998, US)
Kiss of the Vampire, The (Don Sharp,1963, UK)
Lake of Dracula [*Noroi no yakata: Chi o sû me*] (Michio Yamamoto, 1971, Japan)
L'Arrivée d'un train en Gare de la Ciotat (Auguste Lumière and Louis Lumière,
    1896, France)
Last Man on Earth, The (Ubaldo Ragona, 1964, Italy/US)
League of Extraordinary Gentlemen, The (Stephen Norrington, 2003, US)
Le Chaudron Infernal (Georges Méliès, 1903, France)
Le Diable Noir (Georges Méliès, 1905, France)
Legend of the 7 Golden Vampires (Roy Ward Baker, 1974, UK/Hong Kong)
Le Manior du Diable (Georges Méliès, 1896, France)
Le Monstre (Georges Méliès, 1903, France)
Lethal Weapon (Richard Donner, 1987, US)
Let the Right One In [*Låt den rätte komma in*] (Tomas Alfredson, 2008, Sweden)
Lifeforce (Tobe Hooper, 1985, UK)
Love at First Bite (Stan Dragoti, 1979, US)
Lost Boys, The (Joel Schumacher, 1987, US)
Lust for a Vampire (Jimmy Sangster, 1971, UK)
Martin (George A. Romero, 1977, US)
Matrix, The (Andy Wachowski and Larry Wachowski,1999, US)
Mr. Vampire [*Geung si sin sang*] (Ricky Lau, 1985, Hong Kong)
Mummy, The (Stephen Sommers, 1999, US)
My Best Friend is a Vampire (Jimmy Huston, 1988, US)
Nadja (Michael Almereyda, 1994, US)
Near Dark (Kathryn Bigalow, 1987, US)
Night of the Living Dead (George A. Romero, 1968, US)
Night Watch [*Nochnoy Dozor*] (Timur Bekmambetov, 2004, Russia)
Nosferatu, A Symphony of Horror [*Nosferatu, eine Symphonie des Grauens*]
    (F. W. Murnau, 1922, Germany)

Omega Man, The (Boris Sagal, 1971, US)
Planet of Blood (Curtis Harrington, 1966, US)
Planet of the Vampires [*Terrore nello spazio*] (Mario Bava, 1965, Italy)
Rabid (David Cronenberg, 1977, Canada)
Red Violin, The [*Le violin rouge*] (François Girard, 1998, Canada/Italy/UK)
Requiem for a Vampire [*Vierges et vampires*] (Jean Rollin, 1971, France)
Return of Count Yorga, The (Bob Kelljan, 1971, US)
Rocky Horror Picture Show, The (Jim Sharman, 1975, UK/US)
'Salem's Lot (Tobe Hooper, 1975, US)
Satanic Rites of Dracula, The (Alex Gibson, 1974, UK)
Scream Blacula Scream (Bob Kelljan, 1973, US)
Shadow of the Vampire (E. Elias Merhige, 2000, UK/US)
Shaft (Gordon Parks, 1971, US)
Son of Dracula (Robert Siodmak, 1943, US)
Spermula (Charles Matton, 1976, France)
Thirst (Ron Hardy, 1979, Australia)
To Wong Foo Thanks for Everything, Julie Newmar (Beeban Kidron, 1995, US)
Twilight (Catherine Hardwicke, 2008, US)
Twins of Evil (John Hough, 1971, UK)
Ultraviolet (Kurt Wimmer, 2006, US)
Underworld (Len Wiseman, 2003, US)
Underworld: Evolution (Len Wiseman, 2006, US)
Underworld: Rise of the Lycans (Patrick Tatopoulos, 2009, US)
Vampire Circus (Robert Young, 1972, UK)
Vampirella (Jim Wynorski, 1996, US)
Vampire Lovers, The (Roy Ward Baker, 1970, UK)
Vampires Anonymous (Michael Keller, 2003, US)
Vampires in Havana [¡*Vampiros en La Habana!*] (Juan Padrón, 1987, Cuba)
Vampyr [*Vampyr - Der Traum des Allan Grey*] (Carl-Theodor Dreyer, 1932,
    France/Germany)
Vampyres (José Ramón Larraz, 1974, UK)
Vampyros Lesbos (Jesús Franco, 1971, West Germany/Spain)
Van Helsing (Stephen Sommers, 2004, US)
Velvet Vampire, The (Stephanie Rothman, 1971, US)
Wisdom of Crocodiles (Po-Chih Leong, 1998, UK)

BIBLIOGRAPHY

Abbott, Stacey (2007) *Celluloid Vampires: Life After Death in the Modern World*. Austin: University of Texas Press.

Ambrico, Alan S. and Lance Svehla (2006) '"The coin of our realm": Blood and Images in *Dracula 2000*', *Journal of Dracula Studies*, 8, 1–9.

Annandale, David (2002) 'Guerrilla Vamping: *Vampyros Lesbos*, the Becoming-Woman of Women and the Unravelling of the Male Gaze', *Paradox*, 17, 257–70.

Arata, Stephen D. (1997) 'The Occidental Tourist: *Dracula* and the Anxiety of Reverse Colonization', in Nina Auerbach and David J. Skal (eds) *Dracula by Bram Stoker*. New York: W. W. Norton, 462–70.

Auerbach, Nina (1995) *Our Vampires, Ourselves*. Chicago: University of Chicago Press.

Barthes, Roland (1972) *Mythologies*. Trans. Annette Lavers. New York: Noonday Press.

Benshoff, Harry (1997) *Monsters in the Closet: Homosexuality and the Horror Film*. Manchester: Manchester University Press.

Berenstein, Rhona (1996) *Attack of the Leading Ladies: Gender, Sexuality, and Spectatorship in Classic Horror Cinema*. New York: Columbia University Press.

Bordwell, David (1981) *The Films of Carl-Theodor Dreyer*. Berkeley: University of California Press.

Burns, Bonnie (1995) '*Dracula's Daughter*: Cinema, Hypnosis, and the Erotics of Lesbianism', in Carla Jay (ed.) *Lesbian Erotics*. New York: New York University Press, 196–211.

Callens, Johan (2006) '*Shadow of the Vampire*: Double Takes on *Nosferatu*', in Freda Chapple and Chiel Kattenbelt (eds) *Intermediality in Theatre and Performance*. Amsterdam: Rodopi, 195–205.

Case, Sue-Ellen (1991) 'Tracking the Vampire', *Differences: A Journal of Feminist Cultural Studies*, 3, 2, 1–20.

Cohen, Jeffrey Jerome (ed.) (1996) *Monster Theory: Reading Culture*. Minneapolis: University of Minnesota Press.

Craft, Christopher (1984) '"Kiss Me with those Red Lips": Gender and Inversion in Bram Stoker's *Dracula*', *Representations*, 8 (Autumn), 107–33.

Davies, Ann (2008) 'Guillermo del Toro's *Cronos*: The Vampire as Embodied Heterotopia', *Quarterly Review of Film and Video*, 25, 395–403.

Deleuze, Gilles and Félix Guattari (1987) *A Thousand Plateaus: Capitalism and Schizophrenia*. Trans. Brian Massumi. Minneapolis: University of Minnesota Press.

Diawara, Manthia and Phyllis R. Klotman (19991) '*Ganja & Hess*: Vampires, Sex, and Addictions', *Black American Literature Forum*, 25, 2 (Summer), 299–314.

Douglass, Mary (2002) *Purity and Danger: An Analysis of the Concepts of Pollution and Taboo*. New York: Routledge.

Dresser, Norine (1989) *American Vampires: Fans, Victims & Practitioners*. New York: W. W. Norton & Co.

DuBois, W. E. B. (1999)*The Souls of Black Folk*. New York: W. W. Norton & Co.

Dyer, Richard (1988) '*Children of the Night*: Vampirism as Homosexuality, Homosexuality as Vampirism', in Susannah Radstone (ed.) *Sweet Dreams: Sexuality, Gender and Popular Fiction*. London: Lawrence & Wishart, 47–72.

Eisner, Lotte H. (1973) *The Haunted Screen: Expressionism in the German Cinema and the Influence of Max Reinhardt*. Trans. Roger Greaves. Berkeley: University of California Press.

Freud, Sigmund (1955) 'The Uncanny', in *The Standard Edition of the Complete Psychological Works of Sigmund Freud*. Vol. XVII. Trans. James Strachey. London: The Hogarth Press, 218–52.

Gelder, Ken (1994) *Reading the Vampire*. London: Routledge.

Genini, Ronald (1996) *Theda Bara: A Biography of the Silent Screen Vamp, with a Filmography*. Jefferson, NC: McFarland.

Grant, Michael (2003) 'The 'Real' and the Abominations of Hell: Carl-Theodor Dreyer's *Vampyr* (1931) and Lucio Fulci's *E tu vivrai nel terrore—L'aldilà* (*The Beyond*, 1981)', *Kinoeye: New Perspectives on European Film*, 3, 2. On-line. Available at: http://www.kinoeye.org/03/02/grant02.php

Grossman, Lev (2009) 'Zombies are the New Vampires', *Time*, 9 April. On-line. Available at: http://www.time.com/time/magazine/article/0,9171,1890384,00.html

Hake, Sabine (1996) 'Self-Referentiality in Early German Cinema', in Thomas Elsaesser (ed.) *A Second Life: German Cinema's First Decades*. Amsterdam: Amsterdam University Press, 237–45.

Halberstam, Judith (1995) *Skin Shows: Gothic Horror and the Technology of Monsters*. Durham: Duke University Press.

Hanson, Ellis (1999) 'Lesbians Who Bite', in Ellis Hanson (ed.) *Out Takes: Essays on Queer Theory and Film*. Durham: Duke University Press, 183–222.

Hogan, David J. (1986) *Dark Romance: Sexuality in the Horror Film*. Jefferson, NC: McFarland.

Humphries, Reynold (2000) 'The Semiotics of Horror: The Case of *Dracula's Daughter*', *Interdisciplinary Journal for Germanic Linguistics and Semiotic Analysis*, 5, 2, 273–89.

Hurley, Kelly (1995) 'Reading Like an Alien: Posthuman Identity in Ridley Scott's *Alien* and David Cronenberg's *Rabid*', in Judith Halberstam and Ira Livingston (eds) *Posthuman Bodies*. Bloomington: Indiana University Press, 203–24.

Jackson, Rosemary (1981) *Fantasy: The Literature of Subversion*. London: Routledge.

Jacobs, Lewis (1968) *The Rise of the American Film: A Critical History*. New York: Teacher's College Press.

Jenkins, Henry (1992) *Textual Poachers: Television Fans & Participatory Culture*. New York: Routledge.

Jenks, Carol (1996) '*Daughters of Darkness*: A Lesbian Vampire Art Film,' in Andy Black (ed.) *Necronomicon: Book One*. London: Creation Books, 22–34.

Jones, Daryl (2002) *Horror: A Thematic History in Fiction and Film*. London: Arnold.

Jones, Ernest (1931) *On the Nightmare*. London: Hogarth Press.

Kalat, David (2002) 'Exoticism and Eroticism in French Horror Cinema: A Brief Introduction to the World of Jean Rollin', *Kinoeye*, 2, 7; http://www.kinoeye.org/02/07/kalat07.php

Kipling, Rudyard (1940) 'The Vampire', in *The Definitive Edition of Rudyard Kipling's Verse*. London: Hodder and Stoughton, 220-21.

Latham, Rob (2002) *Consuming Youth: Vampires, Cyborgs, and the Culture of Consumption*. Chicago: University of Chicago Press.

LeFanu, Sheridan (1999) 'Carmilla', in Robert Tracy (ed.) *In a Glass Darkly*. Oxford: Oxford University Press, 243–319.

Livingston, Ira (1993) 'The Traffic in Leeches: David Cronenberg's 'Rabid' and the Semiotics of Parasitism', *American Imago*, 50, 4. Gale CENGAGE Academic One File. Web. 4 May 2009. http://o-find.galegroup.com.catalog.lib.cmich.edu

Martin, Anya (1991) 'A Conversation with Anne Rice', *Cemetery Dance*, 3, 34–9.

Marx, Karl (1976) *Capital*. Vol. 1. Trans. Ben Fowkes. New York: Penguin.

Matheson, Richard (1995 [1954]) *I Am Legend*. New York: Tom Doherty Associates.

McClelland, Bruce A. (2006) *Slayers and Their Vampires: A Cultural History of Killing the Dead*. Ann Arbor: University of Michigan Press.

Medovoi, Leerom (1998) 'Theorizing Historicity, or the Many Meanings of *Blacula*', *Screen*, 39, 1, 1–21.

Michaels, Lloyd (1998) '*Nosferatu*, or the Phantom of the Cinema', in Andrew Horton, Stuart Y. McDougal and Leo Braudy (eds) *Play It Again, Sam: Retakes on Remakes*. Berkeley: University of California Press, 239–49.

Milne, Tom (1971) *The Cinema of Carl Dreyer*. New York: A. S. Barnes.

Mulvey, Laura (1975) 'Visual Pleasure and Narrative Cinema', *Screen*, 16, 3, 6–18.

Neergaard, Ebbe (1950) *Carl Theodor Dreyer: A Film Director's Work*. London: British Film Institute.

Newman, Kim (1988) *Nightmare Movies: A Critical Guide to Contemporary Horror Films*. New York: Harmony Books.

Pharr, Mary (1999) 'Vampiric Appetite in *I Am Legend*, '*Salem's Lot*, and *The Hunger*', in Leonard G. Heldreth and Mary Pharr (eds) *The Blood is the Life: Vampires In Literature*. Bowling Green, OH: Popular Press, 93–103.

Pirie, David (1977) *The Vampire Cinema*. New York: Crescent Books.

Prince, Stephen (2004) *The Horror Film*. New Brunswick: Rutgers University Press.

Rice, Anne (1976) *Interview With the Vampire*. New York: Ballantine Books.

Roth, Lane (1984) 'Film, Society and Ideas: *Nosferatu* and *Horror of Dracula*', in Barry Keith Grant (ed.) *Planks of Reason: Essays on the Horror Film*. Metuchen, NJ: The Scarecrow Press, 245–54.

Sedgwick, Eve (1985) *Between Men: English Literature and Homosocial Desire*. New York: Columbia University Press.

Skal, David J. (2004) *Hollywood Gothic: The Tangled Web of Dracula From Novel to Stage to Screen*. New York: Faber and Faber.

Stoker, Bram (1997 [1897]) *Dracula*. Edited by Nina Auerbach and David J. Skal. New York: W. W. Norton & Co.

Stone, Allucquère Rosanne (1995) *The War of Technology and Desire at the Close of the Mechanical Age*. Cambridge, MA: MIT Press.

Todorov, Tzetvan (1973) *The Fantastic: A Structuralist Approach to a Literary Genre*. Trans. Richard Howard. Ithaca, NY: Cornell University Press.

Twitchell, James (1985) *Dreadful Pleasures: An Anatomy of Modern Horror*. New York: Oxford University Press.

Weinstock, Jeffrey Andrew (2001) 'Circumcising Dracula', *Journal of the Fantastic in the Arts*, 12, 1, 90–102.

Weiss, Andrea (1993) *Vampires & Violets: Lesbians in Film*. New York: Penguin.

Welter, Barbara (1985) *The Dimity Convictions: The American Woman in the Nineteenth Century*. Athens, OH: Ohio University Press.

Williams, Linda (1983) 'When the Woman Looks', in Mary Ann Doane, Patricia Mellencamp and Linda Williams (eds) *Re-Visions: Essays in Feminist Film Criticism*. Frederick, MD: University Publications/American Film Institute, 83–99.

Williamson, Milly (2005) *The Lure of the Vampire: Gender, Fiction and Fandom from Bram Stoker to Buffy*. London: Wallflower Press.

Wood, Robin (1974) 'Carl Dreyer', *Film Comment*, March–April, 10–17.

_____ (1985) 'An Introduction to the Horror Film', in Bill Nichols (ed.) *Movies and Methods: An Anthology*. Vol. II. Berkeley: University of California Press, 195–220.

Wright, Richard (2003 [1940]) *Native Son*. New York: HarperCollins.

Zimmerman, Bonnie (1996) '*Daughters of Darkness*: The Lesbian Vampire on Film', in Barry Keith Grant (ed.) *The Dread of Difference: Gender and the Horror Film*. Austin: University of Texas Press, 379–87.

Žižek, Slavoj (2002) *For They Know Not What They Do: Enjoyment as a Political Factor*. London: Verso.

INDEX

Milton Keynes UK
Ingram Content Group UK Ltd.
UKHW030417241024
449966UK00004B/65

9 780231 162012